Colección Támesis

SERIE A: MONOGRAFÍAS, 240

A COMPANION TO SPANISH AMERICAN *MODERNISMO*

ANÍBAL GONZÁLEZ

A COMPANION TO SPANISH AMERICAN *MODERNISMO*

TAMESIS

First published 2007
by Tamesis, Woodbridge

Transferred to digital printing

ISBN 978-1-85566-145-5 hardback
ISBN 978-1-85566-215-5 paperback

Tamesis is an imprint of Boydell & Brewer Ltd
PO Box 9, Woodbridge, Suffolk IP12 3DF, UK
and of Boydell & Brewer Inc.
668 Mt Hope Avenue, Rochester, NY 14620, USA
website: www.boydellandbrewer.com

A CiP catalogue record for this book is available from the British Library

This publication is printed on acid-free paper

CONTENTS

1

The *Modernista* Age

Modernismo was a literary movement of fundamental importance to Spanish America and Spain, which took place over a period of forty years at the turn of the nineteenth century, roughly from the 1880s to the 1920s. Not to be confused with the Brazilian *modernismo* of the 1920s, which corresponds to the European Avant-Garde or to English-language Modernism, Spanish American *modernismo* is widely regarded as the first Spanish-language literary movement to have originated in the New World and to have become influential in the "Mother Country," Spain. Although the splendor of *modernista* poetry is still one of its most admired aspects, *modernismo* is now understood as a broad movement whose impact was felt just as strongly in the prose genres: the short story, the novel, the essay, and the journalistic subgenre of the *crónica* (chronicle). In general terms, it was characterized by the appropriation of French Symbolist aesthetics into Spanish-language literature. However, other significant traits were its cultural cosmopolitanism, its philological concern with language, literary history, and literary technique, and its journalistic penchant for novelty and fashion. These traits also led *modernista* writers to link their work to the changes taking place in music (from Wagner through Debussy), architecture (from Viollet-le-Duc to Gaudí), and the visual arts (Impressionism to Art Nouveau), and this may to a certain extent justify considering *modernismo* as the Spanish American manifestation of an early Modernism, a sort of prelude to the Avant-Garde.

Nevertheless, while Symbolism was but an episode in the development of nineteenth-century French literature, Spanish American *modernismo* was "a literature of foundation," to use a phrase by the contemporary Mexican poet Octavio Paz,[1] a moment when Spanish American writers and intellectuals set out to deliberately create a literature that would be

[1] Octavio Paz, "Literatura de fundación," in *Puertas al campo* (Mexico, Universidad Nacional Autónoma de México, 1966), pp. 11–19.

just as solid and aesthetically valuable as that of their European counterparts. The *modernistas* were well aware of the boldness of their move, for it was a bid by writers from nations that were still striving towards modernity in other spheres, to achieve full literary modernity.

"In everyone the new blood boils," wrote one of the founders of *modernismo*, the Cuban José Martí (1853–95), in a visionary 1882 essay in which he took note of the quickening pace of social and intellectual change:

> There are no permanent works, because works produced during times of realignment and restructuring are shifting and unsettled in their very essence: there are no established paths. … Today, there is a kind of dismantling of the human mind. Gone are the days of high fences; now is the time of broken fences. Now men are beginning to walk across the whole earth without stumbling; before now, they had hardly begun to move when they ran into the wall of a gentleman's estate or the ramparts of a convent. … Cities have more tongues now than there are leaves on the trees of the forest; ideas mature in the public square where they are taught and passed from hand to hand. Speech is not a sin, but a gala occasion; listening is not heresy, but a pleasure, a habit, and a style. The ears are ready for anything; thoughts have hardly sprung up when they are already laden with flowers and fruit and leaping off the page and penetrating every mind like a fine, rarefied dust. Trains vanquish the wilderness; newspapers, the human wilderness. Sunlight penetrates the fissures in old tree trunks. All is expansion, communication, contagion, diffusion.[2]

In a similar vein, the Mexican *modernista* Manuel Gutiérrez Nájera (1859–95), a good friend of Martí's, wrote an essay in 1894 about the value of "miscegenation in literature":

> The aversion to anything foreign, to all that is not of "Old Christian" stock has always been harmful to Spain: suffice it to recall the expulsion of the Jews. It is wrong to say that the Sun never sets on the dominion of our former metropolis: the Sun rises and sets in many countries and it is convenient to try to see all that it shines upon. Let each race preserve its essential characteristics; but it should not isolate itself from others, nor reject others, unless it wishes to shrivel up and die. Free trade is good for intellectual commerce.
>
> The more prose and poetry Spanish literature imports from

2 José Martí, "Prologue to Juan Antonio Pérez Bonalde's *Poem of Niagara*," in *Selected Writings*, ed. Roberto González Echevarría, trans. Esther Allen (New York: Penguin Classics, 2002), pp. 44–6.

> Germany, France, England, Italy, and North and South America, the more literature it will produce and its export products will be richer and more numerous. Literary people may grumble at my use of these plebeian commercial terms, but I find no others in which I can better translate my thoughts.[3]

It was, however, a major *modernista* from a younger generation, the Nicaraguan Rubén Darío (born Félix Rubén García Sarmiento, 1867–1916), who definitively coined the movement's name in 1890, alluding to "the new spirit that today moves a small but triumphant and proud group of writers and poets of Spanish America: *modernismo.*"[4] In that same text, Darío began to define the movement as "freedom and lightness, and the triumph of beauty over precepts in prose; and novelty in poetry: giving color and light and air and flexibility to the ancient verse forms that suffered from paralysis after being tightly imprisoned in iron molds" (Jiménez, 15–16).

Along with the *modernistas*' awareness of the worldwide changes brought about by modernity and their willingness to partake of those changes, something else shines through in these three quotes: a sense of optimism and possibility. To understand the origins of *modernismo* it must be kept in mind that the Spanish America in which this movement arose was no longer the convulsed continent of earlier generations. By the late 1870s the civil strife that had riven the region since Independence in 1810 had come to an end and a period of national consolidation had set in. Throughout the latter part of the nineteenth century, Spanish American urban life becomes more Europeanized as prosperity again comes to the upper and middle classes. The great urban centers of the region, from Mexico City to Santiago, Valparaíso, and Buenos Aires, begin a period of continued growth, reflected in street paving, the construction of broad avenues and boulevards in the style of Paris, and numerous commercial and civic buildings, from banks to opera houses. Technological improvements such as gas lighting and tramways make city life safer and more comfortable. Railway systems, built mostly to link production centers with seaports, nevertheless make travel to the interior of countries such as Argentina, Chile, and Mexico less difficult. The arrival of steamships

[3] Manuel Gutiérrez Nájera, "El cruzamiento en literatura," in *Obras. Crítica literaria,* I (Mexico: Universidad Nacional Autónoma de México, 1959), p. 102. All translations are mine, save where otherwise indicated.

[4] Cited in José Olivio Jiménez, *Antología crítica de la poesía modernista* (Madrid: Ediciones Hiperión, 1985), p. 15.

after the 1850s allows faster and more reliable travel between North and South America and Europe. Immigration from European countries such as Spain and Italy is a significant factor in the growth of many urban centers, particularly in the Southern Cone region, and on the whole the population of Spanish America grows at an impressive rate: for instance, by 1875 Argentina's population had tripled since the beginning of the century, Chile's had doubled, and Mexico's had grown by half.[5]

As historians note, much of this progress was concentrated in the region's urban centers at the expense of the countryside, where large landed estates and mining concerns continued to exploit landless peasants in debt servitude. The social tensions created by this gross inequality were held in check in most countries in the region either by dictatorships with pretensions of enlightened despotism, such as that of Porfirio Díaz in Mexico (which lasted from 1876 to 1911), or by democracies with an elitist and authoritarian cast, in countries such as Argentina and Chile.

It is well to remember, of course, that modernity, both as a nascent concept and as a historical experience, has been present in Spanish American life since the Conquest and is present in the very notion of the Americas as a "New World." Spanish America, however, has more often than not been at the "receiving end" of the modern systems of economic exploitation generated by Europe. This condition of being a passive servant of modernity has often created the impression that Spanish America is not modern at all. From the time of Independence, writers and thinkers in the newly created republics of the region devoted themselves to analyzing the causes of Spanish America's presumed lack of a modern spirit and how to remedy it. Thus, throughout the nineteenth century there arose in Spanish America a series of discourses addressing not only the problem of the existence of a Spanish American modernity but also the possibility of making that modernity a reality. On the one hand, there were works of historiography and political analysis, from Lucas Alamán's *Disertaciones sobre la historia de México* (Dissertations on the History of Mexico, 1844–52) to the Cuban José Antonio Saco's *Historia de la esclavitud* (History of Slavery, 1875–92). On the other, there were the diverse literary or quasi-literary texts that obliquely reflected the modernizing project. This category includes not only those patriotic odes that were, in Rubén Darío's exasperated judgment, "an eternal song to Junín, an endless ode

[5] For the information about Latin American urban development and demographics contained in this paragraph I have relied on Tulio Halperin Donghi, *Historia contemporánea de América Latina* (Madrid, Alianza Editorial, 1975), pp. 210–11, 220–1.

to the agriculture of the torrid zone,"[6] but also such deeply felt and deeply thought out texts as Esteban Echeverría's short story "El matadero" (The Slaughterhouse, 1839), Domingo F. Sarmiento's *Facundo: Civilization and Barbarism* (1854), and Cirilo Villaverde's *Cecilia Valdés* (1879). All of these texts have in common the fact that they are, to a greater or lesser extent, pleas, proposals, or programs geared towards establishing modernity in Spanish America.

Modernismo may well be regarded as the last of the discourses on Spanish America's modernity produced by the nineteenth century, and its very name signals a shift in attitude towards the problem of modernity in Spanish America. Instead of speaking about the need to be modern, the *modernistas* wrote literary works based on the presupposition that *they already were modern*. Modernity, at least for the early *modernistas*, was irreversible and irrevocable: it was their destiny. Buttressed by this sense of historical inevitability, and, of course, by the real instances of socio-economic modernization I have alluded to, the *modernistas* set out to overcome once and for all – at least, at the cultural level – Spanish America's perceived lack of modernity.

Were the *modernistas* really able do this? How could *modernismo* live up to its promise of modernity? Critics of diverse ideological tendencies have proposed a variety of answers: some, such as the Uruguayan Marxist Ángel Rama and his numerous epigones, disturbed by the fact that some of the *modernistas* seemed to have turned their backs on politics and society in order to write highly ornate "ivory tower" poetry and prose, declared that *modernismo* was nothing but a vain effort by intellectually colonized writers to mimic the cultural productions of the European metropolis.[7] For critics like Rama, *modernismo*'s modernity is a failed one, or as one of Rama's disciples more charitably puts it, it is a "divergent modernity."[8] Leftist critics with a more appreciative view of *modernista* writings sought instead to establish a connection between *modernismo* and the socio-economic modernization taking place in the urban milieus where all the *modernistas* lived and worked. Argentine critic Noé Jitrik, for instance, suggested that *modernismo*'s modernity resides in its attempt to imitate, at the textual level, some of the key traits of modern systems of produc-

6 Rubén Darío, *Obras completas*, vol. 1 (Madrid: Afrodisio Aguado, 1950), p. 206.

7 Ángel Rama, *Rubén Darío y el modernismo (Circunstancia socioeconómica de un arte americano)* (Caracas: Universidad Central de Venezuela, 1970), p. 125.

8 Julio Ramos, *Divergent Modernities: Culture and Politics in Nineteenth-Century Latin America*, trans. John D. Blanco (Durham, NC: Duke University Press, 2001).

tion (of capitalist manufacturing, to be exact).[9] According to Jitrik, the *modernistas*' fascination with industrial machinery led them to try to turn their writing into a textual analogue of the machines. The *modernistas* thus created a "semiotic machine," a system of rules and stylistic conventions governing *modernista* writing that ensured the production of poetic texts of consistently high quality. The *modernistas*, in this view, were a sort of enterprising "literary bourgeoisie" who tried to enhance the status of Spanish American literature by imitating the mechanism of capitalist manufacturing.

A more sophisticated if also more abstract view was that proposed by Octavio Paz. Paz posits that *modernismo*'s modernity resides in its embrace of the modern tradition of deep, often revolutionary philosophical criticism. *Modernismo* is modern not only because it tries to imitate the social, political, and cultural institutions of modernity, but also because it explicitly or implicitly critiques them, and even casts a self-critical eye upon its own modernity:

> Antimodern modernity, ambiguous rebellion, *modernismo* was an antitraditionalism and, in its first epoch, an anti-Hispanism – a negation of a certain Spanish tradition. I say a *certain* because at a second moment the *modernistas* discovered the other, the true Spanish tradition. Their admiration for all things French was a kind of cosmopolitanism: Paris was for them, more than a nation's capital, the center of a new esthetic. Cosmopolitanism led them to discover other literatures and to reevaluate our indigenous past. Their exaltation of the pre-Hispanic world was above all an aesthetic one, of course, but it was also something more: it was a critique of modernity and particularly of progress in the style of North America.[10]

Paz's view is by far the most persuasive because it does not seek to diminish the *modernistas*' enormous accomplishments. Furthermore, he correctly identifies the Enlightenment tradition as the ideological source for *modernismo*'s modernity. Paz, however, glosses over precisely how it was that the *modernistas* came into contact with that critical philosophical tradition and transformed it into an aesthetic vision. Paz's insights, in my view, can be complemented by the ideas of the twentieth-century French theorist Michel Foucault. Foucault's work reminds us that the experience

[9] Noé Jitrik, *Las contradicciones del modernismo: productividad poética y situación sociológica* (Mexico: El Colegio de Mexico, 1978).

[10] Octavio Paz, *Los hijos del limo. Del romanticismo a las vanguardias* (Barcelona: Seix-Barral, 1986), p. 6.

of modernity was mediated by a series of institutions and discourses with which the *modernistas* came into direct contact – institutions that served as bridges between the more "concrete" socioeconomical realm and the "abstract" realm of literary production. Chief among these were philology, journalism, and literature. *Modernista* writing can be productively visualized as existing within a triangular field whose boundaries are marked by these three discourses, which, as the nineteenth century wore on, became progressively more institutionalized, that is, embodied in universities, newspapers, and literary circles (often associated with literary journals), and in the practices fostered by these organizations.

Philology, "la *science exacte* des choses de l'esprit" ("the *exact science* of matters of the spirit") as the French philologist Ernest Renan defined it,[11] particularly in the form of literary criticism, was the means through which the *modernistas* became acquainted with the modern way of making literature. Needless to say, the *modernistas*, who were voracious readers, also read directly from the major and minor European writers of the past and present, but it was philology, an already well established modern discipline of textual analysis, which helped them assimilate their readings in a coherent fashion. As Foucault has pointed out, "literature is the refutation of philology (which is, nevertheless, its twin): it submits the language of grammar to the raw power of speech and thus discovers the savage and imperious nature of words."[12] Few *modernistas* would have disagreed with this observation, nor with Renan's assertion that "the modern spirit, that is to say, rationalism, criticism, liberalism, was founded on the same day as philology. *The founders of the modern spirit are the philologists*."[13] Philology, as systematized by the Frenchmen Renan and Hippolyte Taine, as well as by the Spaniard Marcelino Menéndez Pelayo, with its encyclopedic cosmopolitanism, its vision of cultural renewal through the study of history, its interest in religion, and above all its notion of language as an object, as a thing endowed with a concreteness and history of its own, was one of the *modernistas*' chief models for their literary endeavor. Their knowledge of philology linked the *modernistas* with the most advanced and radical thinking about language and literature that Europe had produced so far. Their familiarity with the main figures and ideas of philology is clearly evidenced in the numerous testimonies found in the *modernistas*' essays and journalistic writings. Extensive citations from works by Renan,

[11] Ernest Renan, *L'Avenir de la science. Pensées de 1848* (Paris: Calmann-Lévy, 1890), p. 143.

[12] Michel Foucault, *Les Mots et les choses* (Paris: Gallimard, 1966), p. 313.

[13] Renan, p. 22. Renan's italics.

Taine, Menéndez Pelayo, and the Colombians Miguel Antonio Caro and Rufino José Cuervo, for example, are to be found in the prose writings of most of the major *modernistas*, from Martí and Darío to the Peruvian Manuel González Prada (1848–1918) and the Uruguayan José Enrique Rodó (1872–1917).[14]

The influence of philology on *modernismo* joins with that of another modern institution that gradually and successfully contested philology's claims to authority and relevance: journalism. Virtually all *modernistas* worked as journalists at some point in their careers, since the growth of the urban centers in Spanish America was paralleled by the rise of large, mass-market newspapers such as the venerable *El Comercio* (founded 1839) in Lima, *La Nación* (founded 1870) in Buenos Aires, *La Opinión Nacional* (1870–92) in Caracas, and *El Monitor del Pueblo* (1885–93) in Mexico City. The lack of publishing houses in late nineteenth-century Spanish America made journalism the only regular outlet for literary production. Moreover, their work as journalists satisfied the *modernistas*' desire to become professional writers by allowing them to make a living from writing. Journalism, however, probably taught the *modernistas* far more than they would have wanted to know about writing. Like philology, journalism makes use of texts in its daily activity, and it also aspires to an empirical understanding of the world. Nevertheless, while philology regards texts as objects of knowledge, journalism considers them merchandise; while philology seeks to produce a totalizing synthesis from textual analysis, journalism only seeks to capture the instant, the fleeting moment, in all its empirical detail, without attempting a synthesis. In addition, journalism undermines the idea of the "author" – so vital to nineteenth century literature and philology – because what matters most in journalism is information itself and not the individual who transmits it. In the end, journalism led the *modernistas* to realize that – philological dogma notwithstanding – writing is not a transcendental activity, and that literature, like the other arts, has no "essence," that it is, in Kant's phrase in his *Critique of Judgment* (1790), "purposiveness without purpose."[15]

The *modernistas*' acquaintance with philology and their participation in journalism, along with the general trend toward institutionalization in nineteenth-century society, also led them to regard literature as an institu-

[14] For specific examples and a more detailed discussion of the link between *modernismo* and philology, see Aníbal González, *La crónica modernista hispanoamericana* (Madrid, José Porrúa Turanzas, 1983), pp. 5–59.

[15] *Immanuel Kant's Werke*, vol. 5, ed. Ernst Cassirer (Berlin, Cassirer, 1912–18), p. 291.

tion, with its own coherent rules, standards of quality, and general code of behavior of its members. Their main model for literature as an institution came from French literature, traditionally one of the most institutionalized in Europe, with its schools, cenacles, and academies. As their prose reveals, however, the *modernistas* were far from being the mere imitators of their French models they were often accused of being. (In any case, it is questionable whether one can speak of "imitation" from one language to another, and the *modernistas* were certainly more than just translators.) Their relationship with French literature and culture was analogous to that of the Spanish authors Garcilaso de la Vega, Juan Boscán, and Fernando de Herrera with Italian literature during the sixteenth century; they studied, analyzed, and critically assimilated certain elements of foreign literatures as a means of renewing their own. From the literature of their European counterparts, the *modernistas* learned, above all, to subvert philology by using words with an awareness not only of their etymology but also of their musicality. Words were thus turned from historically determined objects of knowledge into objects of pleasure which could be collected and combined anachronistically, in a "very ancient and very modern way" (as Darío stated in *Cantos de vida y esperanza* [1905]), like pieces of bric-à-brac upon a shelf. One of Martí's meditations on how to uncover the power of words may be seen as emblematic of the way most *modernistas* used the insights of philology to create a new poetic language:

> Words are enveloped by a layer of use; it is necessary instead to seek out their bodies. In this search, it feels as if something is breaking and one can see into the depths. Words must be used just as they appear in their depths, in their real, etymological, and primitive meaning, which is the only robust one, which ensures that ideas expressed in them will last. Words must be resplendent like gold, light like wings, solid like marble.[16]

It is important to recall that *modernismo* was in many ways a liminal phenomenon; that it was, as Martí insisted in his previously cited essay of 1882, an art of transition in an age of transition. This helps to explain why *modernista* writing displays aspects that are clearly modern along with others that seem disconcertingly close to our own "postmodern" times. An example of the former is *modernismo*'s presupposition that there is a profound unity and harmony to the cosmos. In this respect the *modernistas*

16 José Martí, *Obras completas*, vol. 21 (Havana, Editorial Nacional de Cuba, 1963–65), p. 61.

echoed what the twentieth-century French theorist Jean-François Lyotard called the *grand récits*,[17] the great explanatory narratives of nineteenth-century Western philosophy, from G. W. F. Hegel's *Phenomenology of the Spirit* (1807), to Auguste Comte's *Cours de philosophie positive* (1830–53), to Karl Marx's *Das Kapital* (1867–94). On the other hand, *modernista* texts also presuppose that most, if not all, of human knowledge has already been codified amd collected in a single place: in other words, *modernista* writing presupposes the existence of a Library. The metaphor of the Library, which is shared by both literature and philology, is an aspect of *modernista* writing that prefigures postmodernism (witness its use by such Spanish American icons of postmodern literature as Jorge Luis Borges and Gabriel García Márquez).[18] The Library is emblematic of the *modernistas*' lack of interest in originality for its own sake, but, most importantly, it stands for an ideal plane, a kind of intertextual no-man's-land, where philological and literary texts jostle each other and where their placement within an arbitrary scheme (in alphabetical order, for instance) neutralizes their delicate interplay of similarities and differences. The Library not only allows access to a fund of knowledge, but also allows that knowledge to be borrowed and used in an eclectic manner. *Modernismo* was, to a large extent, the appropriation and partial reorganization of the Library of European culture by Spanish America.

As was said at the beginning, the *modernista* movement spanned a period of approximately forty years. It was long-lasting compared with the Avant-Garde movements that would follow it, and indeed, its legacy is arguably still relevant to today's Spanish American literature, as will be discussed in the final chapter of this book. An historical overview of its growth and development will allow us to introduce many of the major authors and works of this movement, as well as some of its main themes and concerns.

The first group of prominent *modernistas* arose independently of each other in different countries of Spanish America and under different circum-

[17] Jean-François Lyotard, *The Postmodern Condition: A Report on Knowledge*, trans. Geoff Bennington and Brian Massumi (Minneapolis: University of Minnesota Press, 1984), pp. 27–37.

[18] For example, in Borges's celebrated story "The Library of Babel" (in *Ficciones*, 1944) and in the Gypsy Melquíades's study in García Márquez's *One Hundred Years of Solitude* (1967). See also Michel Foucault's essay "Fantasia of the Library," in *Language, Counter-Memory, Practice: Selected Essays and Interviews by Michel Foucault*, ed. Donald F. Bouchard (Ithaca, NY: Cornell University Press, 1977), pp. 87–109.

stances. José Martí was a political exile from his native Cuba, who spent nearly half his life traveling in Spain, Venezuela, and Mexico, and in New York City. Manuel Gutiérrez Nájera was a popular middle-class journalist who never traveled far from his beloved Mexico City. José Asunción Silva (1865–96) was a well-to-do Colombian whose family business (a store that sold luxury goods) took him to Paris in 1885, where he frequented literary salons and became something of a dandy. Julián del Casal (1868–93) was a Cuban journalist and minor bureaucrat, whose aristocratic family had fallen on hard times and whose planned trip to Paris only took him as far as Madrid, after which he returned to his native Havana, never to leave it. In time, these four founders of *modernismo* (as most critics now view them) would read each other's works and some would eventually get to meet each other in person.

To a large extent, Martí was the guiding spirit and the principal link between these and other writers of the nascent movement. Born in Havana to Spanish parents of modest origins (his father, a Valencian, was an artillery sergeant in the Spanish Army), Martí absorbed and developed his political views under the tutelage of a Cuban patriot and teacher, Rafael María de Mendive. By 1871, his activities against Spanish colonialism in Cuba had led to his deportation to Spain, where he completed his studies in law and philosophy at the University of Zaragoza. While still in exile, he moved to Mexico (he was there from 1875 to 1877), where he collaborated in the *Revista Universal*, and became a close friend of Manuel Gutiérrez Nájera. Their friendship would endure until both men's deaths in 1895. After periods spent in Cuba, Guatemala, and New York, Martí lived in Venezuela for a year (1881), where he collaborated in the daily *La Opinión Nacional* and founded the *Revista Venezolana*, but soon fell foul of that country's dictatorial government. Back in New York in 1882, Martí published his first book of verses, *Ismaelillo*, which garnered him wide recognition and exemplified the *modernistas*' new poetry. At the same time, he began to write from New York his *crónicas* for the Argentine daily *La Nación*, which were widely reprinted throughout Spanish America. In 1891, after serving as Uruguay's delegate to an International Monetary Conference in New York, he published his second book of poetry, which would also be the last he published during his lifetime, the influential *Versos sencillos* (Simple Verses). By then, Martí had become the undisputed leader of the revolutionary movement to free Cuba and Puerto Rico from Spanish rule, and his activities, although still wide-ranging (as a journalist, public speaker, and consular officer in New York for several Spanish American countries), centered ever more strongly on the Cuban struggle for independence. It was in that struggle, upon his first return to Cuba in almost twenty years, that he died in 1895.

By the time of his death, Martí had already become, by virtue of his popular journalistic writings, a Pan-American celebrity. His restless and intense life, which combined a deeply felt nationalism with a highly refined and cosmopolitan approach to culture and the arts in general, had a profound effect on the Spanish American writers of his own and of younger generations. Silva and Casal, for example, who never met Martí personally, got to know and admire him through his *crónicas* and his books of poetry. With quite a bit of self-interest, Rubén Darío would remember in his autobiography how in his first personal encounter with the Cuban poet in New York in 1893 Martí embraced him and called him "¡Hijo!" ("Son!"), seemingly anointing Darío as his poetic successor. Because of its vivid and compact portrait of Martí and his context, it is worth quoting this passage in full:

> [In New York] I lodged in a Spanish hotel, called Hotel América, and from there the news of my arrival spread throughout the Spanish American community of that imperial city. The first one who came to visit me was a young Cuban, verbose and sociable, with thick black hair, lively and searching eyes and gentlemanly and communicative demeanor. His name was Gonzalo de Quesada, and today he is Cuba's ambassador to Berlin. His long record of Pan-American diplomacy is well known. He told me that the Cuban community was readying a banquet for me at the home of the famous restaurateur Martín, and that the "Maestro" wanted to see me as soon as possible. The "Maestro" was José Martí, who was in those days involved in some of the most difficult moments of his revolutionary work. Gonzalo added that Martí expected me that evening in Harmand Hall, where he was to deliver a speech before a Cuban audience, and that we could go together. I highly admired the vigor of that unique writer, whom I had known through those remarkable and lyrical correspondences he sent to Spanish American dailies such as *La Opinión Nacional* in Caracas, *El Partido Liberal* in Mexico, and, above all, *La Nación* in Buenos Aires. He wrote an abundant prose, full of vitality and color, of plasticity and music. One could clearly see in it his study of the classics and his knowledge of all literatures ancient and modern, and, above all, the spirit of a great and marvelous poet. I arrived punctually to my appointment, and as night fell I entered along with Gonzalo de Quesada by one of the side doors of the building where the great fighter was to speak. We crossed through a dark hallway and suddenly, in a room filled with light, I found myself in the arms of a

> man small in body, with the face of an enlightened one and a voice at once sweet and commanding, who greeted me with a single word: ¡Son![19]

As may be seen, travel among the countries of the Americas and also to Europe was one of the unifying activities of the *modernistas*, enabling them not only to meet each other but also to come into direct contact with other languages and cultures. Another activity that clearly served as a "connective tissue" of sorts for the *modernistas* was journalism. The abundant *crónicas* penned by Martí and Nájera during the 1880s and 1890s, which were frequently reprinted by newspapers in other countries, not only helped to make these writers known abroad, but were also imitated by lesser figures, thus producing a sort of cascading effect through which the developing *modernista* aesthetics became still more widely disseminated.

Critics have usually divided *modernismo* into two periods or stages, separated by the Spanish–Cuban–American War of 1898. In one commonly held view, the writings of the *modernistas* before 1898 (with the notable exception of Martí) are considered more aestheticist, frivolous, and less overtly political than after the war, when there arose a renewed sense of nationalism and Pan-Hispanic solidarity with Spain against "the Colossus of the North" (the United States). This presumed divide between an "Art for Art's Sake" *modernismo* before 1898 and a politically commited one afterwards has recently been called into question by critics who point out the existence of significant political and social concerns in the works of the early *modernistas* besides Martí, particularly when their *crónicas* and other prose writings are taken into account.[20]

It is true, however, that issues of artistic form and the cultural problematics of "decadence" are front and center in the work of most of the early *modernistas*, including Martí. Silva and Casal were particularly interested in the so-called Decadent art and literature of the later French Symbolists, from the poetry of Paul Verlaine and Arthur Rimbaud to novels such as Joris Karl-Huysman's *À rebours* (Against the Grain, 1884), which for many became a handbook of Decadent attitudes and ideas. Decadence, as scholars have long recognized, was essentially an artistic critique of

19 Darío, *Obras completas*, vol. 1, p. 99.

20 See Cathy L. Jrade, *Modernity, and the Development of Spanish American Literature* (Austin: University of Texas Press, 1998); and Gerard Aching, *The Politics of Spanish American* Modernismo*: By Exquisite Design* (Cambridge: Cambridge University Press, 1997).

modernity, and, as such, was itself a modern phenomenon.[21] A great many late nineteenth-century writers and thinkers saw decadence as the inevitable end result of modernity's "progress." After all, nineteenth-century physics, following its discovery of the Second Law of Thermodynamics (also known as "entropy"), posited that the world was moving inevitably towards decrepitude, and sociological treatises such as Brooks Adams's *The Law of Civilization and Decay: An Essay on History* (1895) spoke about the unavoidable decadence of "civilized" societies.[22] For the *modernistas*, the discourse of Decadence was attractive as an expression of their dissidence with regard to Comte's Positivism and its discourse of "progress" that was so prevalent in late nineteenth-century political rhetoric. More significantly, however, Decadentism also allowed some *modernistas*, such as Silva in his novel *De sobremesa* (After-Dinner Talk, 1896) and Darío in the poems of *Prosas profanas* (1896), to critically analyze and reflect about nineteenth-century theories of art and its relation to society, as well as to express the changing sexual mores and the evolving sense of identity of a Spanish American society that was growing ever more diverse and complex.[23]

Nevertheless, there is a real divide of another sort between the first *modernistas* and subsequent members of the movement, and it arises from the coincidence that the four major "founding figures" of *modernismo*, Martí, Nájera, Casal, and Silva all died before 1898. Casal died of tuberculosis in 1893, Martí was killed in battle in 1895, the same year that Nájera died of hemophilia, and Silva took his own life in 1896.

The textual legacy left by that first group of *modernistas* was considerable: aside from the literally hundreds of *crónicas* they wrote, there were innovative short stories such as those by Nájera in *Cuentos frágiles* (Fragile

[21] See the comments by Matei Calinescu in *Five Faces of Modernity: Modernism, Avant-Garde, Decadence, Kitsch, Postmodernism* (Durham, NC: Duke University Press, 1987), pp. 151–195.

[22] Brooks Adams, *The Law of Civilization and Decay: An Essay on History* (New York: Macmillan, 1895).

[23] Recently, readings of *modernismo* in the "Queer Studies" mode have been undertaken, although with mixed results. At their worst, these readings are trivial attempts to show that major *modernistas* were closet homosexuals. The best studies of this kind, however, show how the *modernistas* reflected in their writings about the changing attitudes towards sexual gender and about the relation between sexual gender and literary writing. See, for example, Sylvia Molloy, "La política de la pose," in *Las culturas de fin de siglo en América Latina*, ed. Josefina Ludmer (Rosario: Beatriz Viterbo Editora, 1994), pp. 128–38; and Oscar Montero, "Escritura y perversión en *De sobremesa*," *Revista Iberoamericana*, 178–9 (1997), pp. 249–61.

Stories, 1883), stylized and experimental novels such as Nájera's *Por donde se sube al cielo* (Where One Goes Up to Heaven, 1882), Martí's *Amistad funesta* (also known as *Lucía Jerez*, 1885), and Silva's *De sobremesa*, and of course books of verse with brilliant poems written in a sensuous, ornate, and erudite style not seen in Spanish-language poetry since Spain's Golden Age in the sixteenth and seventeenth centuries: Martí's aforementioned *Ismaelillo* and *Versos sencillos*, Casal's *Nieve* (Snow, 1892), Nájera's posthumously published *Poesías* (1896), and Silva's *El libro de versos* (The Book of Verses) and *Gotas amargas* (Bitter Drops) both published posthumously in 1918. Individual poems by these authors were often published in newspapers and later taken up and declaimed in the "poetic recitals" that were fashionable at the time; thus, often before their publication in a book, many Cubans knew by heart Martí's "Los zapaticos de Rosa" (Rosa's Little Shoes) or some of his *Versos sencillos*, while a good number of Mexicans could recite Nájera's "La Duquesa Job" (The Duchess Job) and virtually all literate Colombians had memorized Silva's haunting "Nocturno."[24]

It is also important to underscore the mentoring and support these early *modernistas* provided for some of their younger colleagues through the literary journals and newspapers they helped to establish. For example, Nájera was co-founder in 1894, with Carlos Díaz Dufóo, of the *Revista Azul*, which became the primary promoter of *modernista* aesthetics in Mexico at the turn of the nineteenth century. Martí, as was already mentioned, founded Venezuela's *Revista Venezolana* in 1881, which also gave prominence to the new literary style. In Cuba, journals founded by *modernista* sympathizers, such as *La Habana Elegante* (1883–96) and *La Habana Literaria* (founded in 1891), gave pride of place in their pages to poets such as Casal. Other journals that were openly sympathetic to *modernismo* during this period were Venezuela's *El Cojo Ilustrado* (1894–1915), Uruguay's *Revista Nacional de Literatura y Ciencias Sociales* (founded by *modernista* essayist José Enrique Rodó in 1895), and, in Buenos Aires, *Revista de América* (1896) founded by Rubén Darío and the Bolivian *modernista* Ricardo Jaimes Freyre (1868–1933), *El Mercurio de América* (1898–1900), and *La Biblioteca* (1896–98) established by the Franco-Argentine literary critic Paul Groussac (1848–1929).[25]

24 See Eduardo Jaramillo-Zuluaga, "Artes de la lectura en la ciudad del águila negra: la lectura en voz alta y la recitación en Santafé de Bogotá a fines del siglo XIX," *Revista Iberoamericana*, 184–5 (1998), pp. 471–83.

25 See Aching's excellent chapter on "Founding a Transnational Cultural Literacy:

The "leadership vacuum" produced by the deaths of the early *modernistas* was swiftly filled by a group of younger and no less enthusiastic writers whose undisputed figurehead was Rubén Darío. For reasons that had much less to do with politics than with his own need to make a living, as well as with his own zeal for promoting the new aesthetic ideas, Darío traveled even more widely than Martí, carrying out for the younger *modernistas* a connective function similar to Martí's. Darío, who would characterize his whole life as a "pilgrimage" without a fixed destination,[26] left his native Nicaragua for Chile in 1886, where he worked in journalism and published his celebrated book of short stories and poems *Azul...* (1888). In 1889 he returned to Nicaragua, and remained in the Central American region until 1892. During those years, he married for the first time, his first son was born, and he published a second revised edition of *Azul...* (1890). In 1892, he traveled to Spain as Nicaragua's envoy to the celebration of the fourth centennial of Columbus's voyage to the New World. In Spain, Darío, who had already achieved poetic renown, was warmly received by many of the "Mother Country's" most relevant intellectuals at the time, from the philologist Menéndez Pelayo to the novelist Emilia Pardo Bazán and the critic Juan Valera.

On his way back to Nicaragua, Darío's steamship stopped briefly in Havana, where he met Julián del Casal. Shortly after his return to his home country in 1893, his first wife died and that same year an inebriated Darío was forced – quite literally – into a "shotgun marriage" with an upper-class Nicaraguan woman, Rosario Murillo. An opportune offer by the Colombian government allowed Darío to escape from the whole sordid business, and soon he was on his way to Buenos Aires as Colombia's consul to that city. Steamship itineraries to Buenos Aires in those days required layovers in New York and the French port of Le Havre; it was during his stay in New York that he met Martí in the episode cited above. A few weeks later, during a brief stay in France, he traveled to Paris, where he met one of his idols, Paul Verlaine (the "unfortunate master," Darío recalls in his memoirs, had been thoroughly drunk, and his only coherent words had been: "*La gloire! ... La gloire! ... M... M... encore! ...*").[27]

The *Modernista* Literary Reviews" in *The Politics of Spanish American* Modernismo, pp. 115–43.

26 One of Darío's collections of his *crónicas* was titled *Peregrinaciones* (Pilgrimages, 1901), and one of his late books of poems was titled, more revealingly, *El canto errante* (The Wandering Song, 1907).

27 Darío, *Obras completas*, vol. 1, pp. 103–4.

As Max Henríquez Ureña points out in his by no means brief *Breve historia del modernismo* (Brief History of *Modernismo*, 1954),

> Darío's stay in Buenos Aires (from 1893 to 1898) ... marks the moment when *modernismo* reaches its apogee. In Argentina Darío found a group of writers and poets who identified themselves with the movement for literary renewal he represented, among which were Ricardo Jaimes Freyre, Luis Berisso, Leopoldo Díaz, Eugenio Díaz Romero, Leopoldo Lugones, Ángel de Estrada, and Alberto Ghiraldo.[28]

During those years in Buenos Aires, Darío published two books that cemented his reputation as the leading *modernista*: the book of essays *Los raros* (The Strange Ones, 1896) and the aforementioned book of poems *Prosas profanas*. It was the latter book which caused the greatest stir, not only because of its sensuous, erotically charged poems, but also because of Darío's prose prologue, which was widely regarded as a manifesto for *modernismo* despite Darío's unconvincing claim in its first lines that "I do not have a literature that is *mine* – as a magisterial authority has said – with which I try to lead others down my same path. My literature is *mine* in me; whoever follows my tracks like a slave will lose his personal treasure."[29]

Darío's tracks would lead him to become something none of his predecessors in *modernismo*, and indeed, no other Spanish American writer before him, had ever been: a truly international celebrity. Martí had very nearly achieved this status, but his single-minded devotion to Cuban independence had led him in the end to focus almost all his strength and his activity on that cause. An essentially apolitical being, Darío had no such limits, and he relished the many banquets given in his honor (these were, after all, "the banquet years," as Roger Shattuck referred to the turn of the nineteenth century),[30] along with the adoring crowds receiving him at the railroad stations or awaiting his speeches in a theater, and the attentions of the famous and powerful people of the age, including not a few dictators (the Nicaraguan José Santos Zelaya and the Guatemalan Estrada Cabrera, among others). With a mixture of self-indulgence and naïveté, even as he was writing poetry that aspired to the sublime, Darío gave himself to the

28 Max Henríquez Ureña, *Breve historia del modernismo* (Mexico: Fondo de Cultura Económica, 1954), pp. 95–6.

29 Rubén Darío, *Prosas profanas* (Madrid, Espasa-Calpe, 1967), p. 10.

30 Roger Shattuck, *The Banquet Years: The Origins of the Avant-Garde in France, 1885 to World War I* (New York: Vintage Books, 1968).

pursuit of earthly pleasures, much as film stars or rock musicians of a later age would do. His alcoholic binges alternated with bouts of regret and self-doubt, and his frequent womanizing would be followed by a return to the motherly embrace of Francisca Sánchez, the illiterate Spanish mistress he met in Madrid in 1899, whom he would refer to as his "lazarillo de Dios" ("blind-person's guide to God").

Like many other great writers before and since, however, Darío was able to transform the increasingly sordid details of his existence into lasting works of literature, such as the book of poems *Cantos de vida y esperanza* (Songs of Life and Hope, 1905), which is in many ways his last great work. The poems in this book take on a pattern that, although consonant with Darío's life experience, would also become something of a literary topic among the *modernistas* during the early years of the twentieth century: confession followed by conversion followed by peregrination. Introspection, self-analysis, a sense of doubt and existential anguish, and a search for certainty couched in religious terminology, are evidenced in much of Darío's later poetry and in that of many of his *modernista* contemporaries.

Darío's turn towards a more introspective, solemn, and in some instances more visibly political poetry, which was echoed by his comrades in *modernismo*, was not solely due to the vagraries of his life as a celebrity. One historical event in particular, the Spanish–Cuban–American War of 1898, marked the life of the Nicaraguan poet as well as that of all other Spanish-speaking intellectuals. This short war, in which the US intervened in Cuba's ongoing struggle for independence from Spain (which had been relaunched by Martí in the 1880s), resulted in the US takeover of Spain's last imperial possessions – Cuba, Puerto Rico, and the Philippines – and was the prelude to decades of aggressive interventionist policies by the US in Latin America. During the early decades of the twentieth century, the US would occupy Panama (1904–14), Nicaragua (1912–25), Haiti (1914–34), the Dominican Republic (1916–24), and Cuba (1917–23). For Spaniards as well as for Spanish Americans, the "catastrophe of 98" would darken their previously hopeful view of the new century and would signal the beginning of a more pessimistic, self-questioning period in their cultural history.

Another event not directly related to the crisis of 1898 also signaled the end of Spanish America's *belle époque*: the Mexican Revolution, which lasted from 1910 to 1920. The ideology of this social upheaval, inasmuch as it had an ideology, was mostly liberal and petit-bourgeois in orientation. Nevertheless, the Mexican Revolution was also deeply rooted in the peasantry, and it effectively tore down the edifice of the dictator Porfirio Díaz's elitist and positivistic regime. During the Revolution, Mexican intellectuals, many of whom were refined humanists, were reduced to working as mere secretaries or advisors to *caudillos* who were often illiterate and of working-class origins, such as Emiliano Zapata and Pancho Villa. The narrative works that resulted from the Mexican Revolution (which constitute a minor literary genre in themselves), from Mariano Azuela's *Los de abajo* (The Underdogs, 1916) to Martín Luis Guzmán's *El águila y la serpiente* (The Eagle and the Serpent, 1928), not only leave many of the trappings of *modernismo* behind, but also testify to a renewed sense of crisis and historical change to which writers and intellectuals needed to adapt.

By the time of Darío's death in Nicaragua in 1916, the torch of *modernismo* had passed to younger writers and once again, as in *modernismo*'s beginning, prose writing heralded the movement's new directions and concerns. Already in 1900, a new *modernista* star had risen with the publication of the essay *Ariel* by José Enrique Rodó. In a prose style that was still ornate and edulcorated in the worst *modernista* fashion, Rodó nevertheless called for a cultural renewal in Spanish America headed by its youth (the essay is tellingly dedicated "*A la juventud de América*," "To the youth of America"). His appeal to Pan-Hispanic unity and activism in the face of US expansionism struck a responsive chord throughout the Spanish-speaking world. Rodó's death in 1917, however, cut short the career of a critic and intellectual who had begun to be regarded by many as a guiding figure in the turbulent early years of the new century.

In its late phase, timidly at first, but with increasing audacity at the end, *modernismo*'s best prose and poetry began striking out towards a more openly experimental attitude that tended to merge with the Avant-Garde. At the same time, it must be said, the *modernista* style was making itself felt within the broader culture of Spanish America, even at the level of popular music. As often happens in cultural history, cultural productions that start off being by and for the elite are later appropriated and transformed by a broader segment of society. This was the case with *modernista* poetry, whose aestheticism was quickly turned into a new standard of taste, adopted even by the middle and working classes, and whose penchant for musicality drew the attention of the popular musicians who catered to those classes. Thus, for example, the originally coarse lyrics of the lower-class tango in Argentina began to mimic the more sophisticated and ornate turns of phrase of *modernista* poetry. In Cuba, the bolero, an entirely new genre of popular music which would take Spanish America by storm, drew inspiration for its lyrics largely from the introspective and sentimental verses of Darío's later years.

Even as the style of *modernismo* was permeating the Spanish Americans' daily lives, some of the *modernistas* became aware of the increased pace of change in culture and the arts in the first decades of the twentieth century. Modernity was once again on the move, and the *modernistas* struggled to keep pace with it. Darío himself had written *crónicas* in which he quizzically regarded the new European Avant-Garde movements, such as Italian futurism.[31] Novelists such as the Venezuelan Manuel Díaz Rodríguez (1871–1927) sought in their novels a sort of "third way" between the extremes of the Frenchman Émile Zola's Naturalism (with its biologically-determined portrayal of society) and Huysman's Decadence, whose pessimistic attitude seemed to lead nowhere. A *modernista* novel such as Díaz Rodríguez's *Ídolos rotos* (Broken Idols, 1901), heavily influenced by the ideas of Rodó, already foreshadows in its very title the iconoclastic attitude that would come to predominate in the new arts. The short stories in *Las fuerzas extrañas* (Strange Forces, 1906) by Leopoldo Lugones (1874–1938), one of the young Argentines Darío had mentored in Buenos Aires, dealt increasingly with themes such as science-fiction and the occult, in an obvious attempt to confront modernity more directly.

The poetry of Lugones and his Uruguayan colleague Julio Herrera y Reissig (1875–1910) grew even more daring. As Gwen Kirkpatrick points out, these poets represent the "dissonant legacy" of *modernismo*.[32] By means of the intensified and parodic use of *modernista* rhetorical devices and themes, these two Southern Cone poets took *modernismo* to its limits, to the very doorstep of the Avant-Garde. A stanza from Herrera y Reissig's "Tertulia lunática" (Lunatic Conversation, 1909) exemplifies his dissolution of *modernismo*'s harmonious poetic language through humor and excess:

> Oh black flower of Idealism!
> Oh hyena of diplomacy,
> with bile of aristocracy
> and blue leprosy of idealism! ...
> Your eroticism is a cancer
> of taciturn absurdity,

31 Darío, *Obras completas*, vol. 1, pp. 616–24.

32 Gwen Kirkpatrick, *The Dissonant Legacy of* Modernismo*: Lugones, Herrera y Reissig, and the Voices of Modern Spanish American Poetry* (Berkeley: University of California Press, 1989).

> and it flourishes in my saturn
> fever of destructive virus,
> like a culture of stars
> in the nocturnal gangrene.[33]

These verses, with their imagery of disease and transformation derived from the sciences (particularly biology and medicine) prefigure the end of *modernismo* as it had been known, and its metamorphosis into the Avant-Garde.

In the chapters that follow, we will examine in greater detail *modernismo*'s broad and profound contribution to the various genres of Spanish American literary production. Keeping in mind the general framework of *modernismo*'s historical development as I have outlined it here, in the next chapters we will trace how *modernismo* took up and transformed previously existing genres as well as creating new ones. We begin in Chapter 2 with a genre of the *modernistas*' own invention, the *crónica*, and the contribution to its development by writers like Nájera, Martí, and the Guatemalan Enrique Gómez Carrillo (1873–1927). Given the *crónica*'s close relationship to the short story genre, in Chapter 3 we proceed to discuss the *modernista* short story, with particular attention to the pioneering stories by Nájera and Darío, as well as the later stories of Lugones, Díaz Rodríguez, and the Uruguayan Horacio Quiroga (1878–1937). Another genre closely linked to the *crónica* as well as to the short story is the *modernista* essay, the subject of Chapter 4, in which we examine works by Martí, Rodó, González Prada, and the Colombian Baldomero Sanín Cano (1861–1957). Chapter 5 deals with the *modernista* novel in both its formal and ideological aspects, covering texts by Nájera, Martí, Silva, Díaz Rodríguez, and the Chilean Pedro Prado (1886–1952). The panorama of *modernista* poetry is quite vast, and in Chapter 6 we offer a broad outline of its major traits and themes as well as specific comments on texts by Martí, Silva, Darío, Lugones, Herrera y Reissig, and *modernismo*'s sole major woman poet, the Uruguayan Delmira Agustini (1886–1914), whose work opened the gates to a much greater number of women poets in the *posmodernista* period. Lastly, in Chapter 7 we consider the question of *modernismo*'s legacy. While it is true that *modernismo*'s creative phase ended long ago (roughly around the 1920s), its foundational echoes are still heard even in today's postmodern Spanish American literature. As will

[33] Cited in. Kirkpatrick, p. 187. Kirkpatrick's translation.

be seen in a brief overview of texts by various contemporary authors such as Miguel Barnet, Jorge Luis Borges, Alejo Carpentier, Gabriel García Márquez, José Lezama Lima, Octavio Paz, and Sergio Ramírez, Spanish American literature still remains enthralled with the relics of its origins in the *modernista* age.

Further Reading

For this and subsequent chapters the best general source books on *modernismo* are:

Aching, Gerard, *The Politics of Spanish American* Modernismo*: By Exquisite Design* (Cambridge: Cambridge University Press, 1997).

Castillo, Homero, ed., *Estudios críticos sobre el modernismo* (Madrid: Gredos, 1968). A wide-ranging anthology of essays by many of the major critics of *modernismo* up to the 1960s.

Davison, Ned J., *The Concept of Modernism in Hispanic Criticism* (Boulder, CO: Pruett Press, 1966). Offers a useful summary of the debates concerning the nature of *modernismo* up to the 1960s.

Gutiérrez Girardot, Rafael, *Modernismo* (Barcelona: Montesinos, 1983).

Henríquez Ureña, Max, *Breve historia del modernismo* (Mexico: Fondo de Cultura Económica, 1978). Despite its title, an extensive, detailed, and highly readable account of *modernismo*'s history in a traditional historico-critical style, including biographical sketches of the major *modernistas* and country by country accounts of *modernismo*'s development. A classic.

Jitrik, Noé, *Las contradicciones del modernismo: productividad poética y situación sociológica* (Mexico: El Colegio de Mexico, 1978). Imaginative and sophisticated readings of *modernista* texts from a sociocritical point of view.

Jrade, Cathy L., Modernismo, *Modernity, and the Development of Spanish American Literature*. (Austin: University of Texas Press, 1998). Elegant, up-to-date account of *modernismo*'s development, especially strong in its discussion of poetic texts.

Paz, Octavio, *Los hijos del limo. Del romanticismo a las vanguardias* (Barcelona: Seix-Barral, 1986). Expanded and revised version of Paz's Charles Eliot Norton lectures at Harvard University in 1972. Classic discussion of *modernismo* in the context of the philosophical debate about modernity and the modern poetic tradition.

Rama, Ángel, *Rubén Darío y el modernismo (Circunstancia socio-económica de un arte americano)* (Caracas: Universidad Central de Venezuela, 1970). Readings of Darío and the *modernistas* inspired by the Frankfurt School of Marxist criticism.

Schulman, Ivan A., *Génesis del modernismo: Martí, Nájera, Silva, Casal* (Mexico: El Colegio de México, 1966). Classic study of the early *modernistas*.

The Cambridge History of Latin American Literature, vol. 2 (Cambridge: Cambridge University Press, 1996). Chapters 1 and 2, by Cathy L. Jrade and Aníbal González, respectively, cover the areas of "Modernist Poetry" and "Modernist Prose."

2

Modernismo and Journalism: The *crónicas*

Crónica is the name given in Spanish to a hybrid genre that combines literary with journalistic elements in a variety of ways, resulting in brief texts that often focus on contemporary topics and issues addressed in a self-consciously literary style. Still a vibrant genre that continues to be practiced today by major Spanish American writers, from Gabriel García Márquez and Mario Vargas Llosa to Elena Poniatowska and Luisa Valenzuela, the *crónica* was created in the Americas by the *modernistas* during the 1870s and 1880s. They were inspired by a similar type of article called *chroniques*, which began to be published in Parisian newspapers such as *Le Figaro* and *La Chronique Parisienne* during the 1850s.[1] In many instances, *crónicas* account for more than two-thirds of the *modernistas*' published writings, as can be seen in the complete works of such major *modernistas* as José Martí, Manuel Gutiérrez Nájera, Rubén Darío, José Enrique Rodó, and the Guatemalan Enrique Gómez Carrillo (1873–1927). Because of their abundance and ubiquity, as well as the high regard the *modernistas* had for them, the *crónicas* may be considered the touchstones, or perhaps even the keystones of *modernista* literary creation in both prose and poetry.

The importance of the *crónicas* for the *modernistas* lies fundamentally in their link with one of modernity's archetypal institutions: journalism. Let us recall that modernity as a sociohistorical concept encompasses, among other things, capitalism and its discontents, representative government, and a belief in the transformative power of technology. In the cultural sphere, modernity is linked to change, to renewal, to the twin ideas of progress and decadence, to historicism, to criticism, and to the presumed provisional character of all socioeconomic and political structures. As the institution charged with producing a written account of these changes,

1 *Histoire générale de la presse française* (Paris: Presses Universitaires de France, 1969), II, pp. 298–302.

journalism became the textual mouthpiece of modernity and one of its principal promoters. The *crónicas*, with their concern with the present, with the "here and now," embodied for the *modernistas* the very essence of textual modernity.

The *crónica modernista* is in fact the heir to a somewhat complicated genealogical tree whose roots are found in the essays of manners of Joseph Addison (1672–1719) and Richard Steele (1672–1729), as well as of French authors such as Jouy (Victor-Joseph Etienne, 1764–1846) and Honoré de Balzac (1799–1850), and Spanish authors such as Mariano José de Larra (1809–37), and whose branches extend to the aforementioned Parisian *chronique*, to the Peruvian Ricardo Palma's (1833–1919) *Tradiciones peruanas* (Peruvian Traditions), and to the first *crónicas* by the Mexican Gutiérrez Nájera in 1875.

However, the *crónicas* were far more than mere residues of the daily work as journalists with which virtually all the major *modernistas* earned their living. They were also the expression of the *modernistas*' conflictive relation with journalism. In 1893, the Cuban *modernista* Julián del Casal voiced in stark terms the *modernistas*' main complaints about the journalistic institution:

> Journalism, as it is understood today among us, is the most nefarious institution for those who, not knowing how to place their pen in the service of petty causes, or disdaining the ephemeral applause of the crowds, are possessed by the love of Art. … The first thing that is done to the journalist when he takes his post in the newspaper office is to deprive him of one of the writer's indispensable attributes: his own personality. … Thus the journalist, from the moment he begins his work, has to suffer through immense avatars according to the demands of his newspaper, turning into a republican if he is a monarchist, into a freethinker if he is a Catholic, or into an anarchist if he is a conservative. I will not mention here the thousand menial chores of journalism, the only ones to which young men of letters can aspire, because it would take me too long to enumerate them. Suffice it to say that some, such as those having to do with the gossip columns, are not only stupefying but also degrading. Journalism can be, in spite of its intrinsic hatred of literature, the benefactor that puts money in our pockets, bread on our table, and wine in our cup, but, alas, it will never be the tutelary deity that encircles our brow with a crown of laurel leaves.[2]

2 Julián del Casal, *Prosas* (Havana: Consejo Nacional de Cultura, 1963), I, p. 272.

According to Casal, journalism undermined the notion of the author's self as a source of authority, and it furthermore turned the literary text from an object of aesthetic contemplation into merchandise. Similar sentiments were echoed by Nájera and Martí. Martí, however, saw clearly that journalism's effects on literature had less to to with its "intrinsic hatred of literature" (as Casal put it) than with modernity and the quickened pace of modern life. In his famous 1882 prologue to the Venezuelan Juan Antonio Pérez Bonalde's (1846–92) "El poema del Niágara" ("The Poem of Niagara"), Martí observed:

> Today there is a kind of dismantling of the human mind. Gone are the days of high fences; this is the time of broken fences. … The ears are ready for anything; thoughts have hardly sprung up when they are already laden with flowers and fruit, and leaping off the page and penetrating every mind like a fine, rarefied dust. Trains vanquish the wilderness; newspapers, the human wilderness. Sunlight penetrates the fissures in old tree trunks. All is expansion, communication, florescence, contagion, diffusion. The newspapers deflower grandiose ideas. Ideas do not form families in the mind, as before, or build homes, or live long lives. … We arise in the morning with one problem, and by the time we go to bed at night we have exchanged it for another. Images devour each other in the mind. There is not enough time to give form to thought.[3]

In the end, their experience in journalism would definitively erode the *modernistas*' old-fashioned ideas about literature as self-expression and about the literary text as a perfectly crafted and coherent artistic creation, thus paving the way for the changes of the Avant-Garde. However, this did not prevent the *modernistas* from striking back in their *crónicas* against the restrictions of journalism. This was done by turning the *crónicas* into a complex, highly protean genre that was not strictly bound by the usual limitations of journalistic discourse. In the *crónicas*, the *modernistas* took every opportunity offered by the institution of the press in order to sharpen their literary skills and to explore and define the nature of literary discourse in contrast with journalistic discourse. The *modernistas* analyzed in the *crónicas* the legacy of Western literature's rhetoric and literary genres and, guided by the principles of historical linguistics and philology, exalted language's rebellious traits and its nature as an autono-

[3] José Martí, "Prologue to Juan Antonio Pérez Bonalde's *Poem of Niagara*," in *Selected Writings*, ed. Roberto González Echevarría, trans. Esther Allen (New York: Penguin Classics, 2002), pp. 44–6.

mous object rather than a mere vehicle for conveying ideas. At the same time, the *modernistas* used the *crónicas* to express their anticapitalist, artisanal vision of artistic creation and tried out the literary possibilities that arose when language was conceived as an object. Thus, despite their dependence on journalism as an institution (in which they were merely salaried employees) the *modernistas* developed in their *crónicas* a decorative and frivolous discourse, chock-full of vivid metaphors and cultural allusions, with which they implicitly defied the informative and utilitarian demands of journalism.

Nevertheless, the *modernista* chronicles continued to display conventionally journalistic traits: usually, *crónicas* take as their point of departure some item of news or some public event which the *cronista* then glosses in a witty and entertaining way. In fact, their value as entertainment is also indicative of another important journalistic trait of the *modernista* chronicles: their nature as merchandise. As the director of the venerable Buenos Aires daily *La Nación*, Bartolomé Mitre y Vedia, reminded José Martí in the 1880s after asking him to tone down the controversial anti-US rhetoric in his *crónicas*:

> Please do not take this letter as the pretentious lesson one writer aims to give another. I am speaking to you as a young man who probably has more to learn from you than you from me. But since we are dealing here with a merchandise – please forgive me for being so brutally frank, but I wish to be exact – that is seeking favorable placement, I am simply trying, as is my duty and my right, to reach an agreement with you as one of my agents and correspondents so as to give it the fullest value it can have.[4]

Crónicas were texts meant to be bought and consumed along with the newspaper in which they appeared, and which therefore needed to contribute to the newspaper's appeal. Not infrequently, as with Nájera and Julián del Casal, *crónicas* were addressed to a predominantly female reading public. Female readers, according to the patriarchal prejudices of the age, could not have their minds burdened with weighty discussions and instead needed to be offered "delicate" products that could be easily consumed. From the beginning there were important exceptions to this rule, however. Many of Martí's *crónicas*, particularly his "Escenas europeas" (European Scenes, 1875–82) and "Escenas norteamericanas" (North

[4] Cited in Gonzalo de Quesada y Miranda, *Martí, periodista* (Havana: Rambla, Bouza, 1929), p. 105.

American Scenes, 1881–84), were equally valuable as news reporting and as literary creations.

The *crónica* offers the clearest illustration of how *modernista* discourse, as I argued in Chapter 1, dwells in the midst of a triangular field bounded by three modern institutions: philology, journalism, and literature. As a journalistic genre, the *crónica* was obliged to convey news of current events and to be subject to the commercial law of supply and demand. As a literary genre, it had to be original and entertaining but it also had to be well written, with a solid philological awareness of the history of language. Evidently, the *crónica* had to be many things at the same time, and this led it to become a genre that mediated among other, sometimes opposite, genres and discourses. Unlike the poetry the *modernistas* wrote with such practiced ease, the *crónica* lacked a unified poetics (that is, a theory of what it was and how it should be written), although, as will be seen shortly in more detail, attempts to produce such a poetics were not lacking, particularly in the works of second-generation *modernista* chroniclers such as Darío and Gómez Carrillo.

Like other *modernista* genres, the *crónica* also evolved throughout the decades in which *modernismo* became a predominant literary movement. The *crónicas* written by the founding generation of *modernistas* (Nájera, Martí, Casal, Silva), despite their often bewildering thematic variety, are in general characterized by a strong subjectivism, that is, by the writer's tendency to observe and describe everything through the prism of the self. As *modernismo* continued to develop, however, the influence of journalism coupled with many of the cultural and political changes summarized in Chapter 1 – from the celebrity status of some *modernistas* to events such as the Spanish–Cuban–American War of 1898 and the Mexican Revolution – led to the rise of a more self-critical approach in the *crónicas* of younger *modernistas* such as Darío, Rodó, and Gómez Carrillo. Significantly, this period also saw the rise of a new form of *crónica*, the *crónica de viajes* or "travel chronicle."

Any discussion of the earliest *crónicas modernistas* must begin with Manuel Gutiérrez Nájera, who is generally credited with introducing the genre of the *crónica* into Spanish American journalism. Inspired by the *chroniques* published in French dailies, during his twenty years in journalism (from 1875 until his sudden death in 1895) Nájera wrote countless *crónicas* for Mexican newspapers such as *El Federalista*, *El Partido Liberal*, *La Libertad*, *El Cronista Mexicano*, and *El Universal*, among many others. None of Nájera's *crónicas* were collected during his lifetime, unless one counts the short stories published in his *Cuentos frágiles*

(Fragile Stories) in 1883, many of which had first appeared in print, in whole or in part, as *crónicas*. Indeed, a purposeful blurring of the line between journalism and fiction is a hallmark of Nájera's work in prose.

Fiction was for Nájera, as for most post-romantic authors, closely allied to subjectivism, to the notion of an inner self. In his *crónicas* Nájera consistently subjectivizes objective phenomena, from natural catastrophes such as an earthquake, in "Crónica color de bitter" (Bitter-colored Chronicle, 1882), to political events, in his *Plato del día* (Daily Special, 1893–95) series.[5] This he does largely by viewing events from the perspective of the turn-of-the-century bourgeois interior, which, as Walter Benjamin reminds us, in his well-known essay "Paris, Capital of the Nineteenth Century" (1935), could be either an office, a bedroom, a library, or a museum.[6] Nájera's interior is, like Benjamin's, a place where the self takes refuge from temporality and history. For Nájera, the temporality of the interior is arbitrary and capricious, subject to the whims of the self, and the interior as a whole is regarded as a space where the self, given free rein, can indulge in hallucinations, games, and erotic pleasures.

Among Nájera's many *crónicas*, "La hija del aire" (The Daughter of the Air, 1882) undoubtedly exemplifies the extremes to which his exploration of subjectivity could go within a journalistic context. First published in the daily *El Nacional* on April 6, 1882, it was later included by Nájera, without modifications, in his *Cuentos frágiles*. The overt theme of this *crónica*, as Nájera states at the end, is a protest against the common nineteenth-century problem, in Mexico and elsewhere, of exploitative child labor practices: "Who will free those poor beings who are corrupted and prostituted by their own parents, those martyred children whose existence is an endless punishment, those unfortunates who travel through the three great infernal circles of life: Sickness, Hunger, and Vice?"[7] Most of this *crónica*'s few pages are devoted to a description of a little girl-acrobat whom the narrator sees at a circus that has come to Mexico City. The narrator begins by telling us of his distaste for circuses, which he sees as places where "human abjection" is on display:

[5] For "Crónica color de bitter," see Manuel Gutiérrez Nájera, *Cuentos, crónicas y ensayos*, ed. Alfredo Maillefert (Mexico: Universidad National Autónoma de México, 1940), pp. 53–8. For the *Plato del día* series, see Manuel Gutiérrez Nájera, *Escritos inéditos de sabor satírico, "Plato del día"*, ed. Boyd G. Carter and Mary Eileen Carter (Columbia, MS: University of Missouri Press, 1972).

[6] Walter Benjamin, "Paris, Capital of the Nineteenth Century," *Reflections: Essays, Aphorisms, Autobiographical Writings* (New York: Schocken Books, 1986), p. 154.

[7] Manuel Gutiérrez Nájera, *Cuentos completos y otras narraciones*, ed. E. K. Mapes (Mexico: Fondo de Cultura Económica, 1958), p. 176.

> I rarely go to the circus. Any spectacle in which I see displayed human abjection, whether moral or physical, is greatly repugnant to me. However, a few nights ago, I entered a tent that was raised in the small plaza near the Seminario. A contortionist dislocated himself with grotesque contortions, exploiting his ugliness, his shamelessness, and his idiocy, like those beggars who, in order to stimulate the expected benevolence of the passerby, display their sores and exploit their rottenness. A woman – almost naked – twisted about like a snake in the wind. Three or four gymnasts muscled like Hercules threw at each other large weights, bronze balls, and iron bars. What degradation! What misery! (*Cuentos completos*, p. 173)

The girl-acrobat who mounts the trapeze is described as an orphan, "daughter of pain and sadness" (*Cuentos completos*, p. 175), a "weak, small, and sickly being" (p. 175) who is prematurely aged, battered by her life in the circus, where the audience "that shouts, that howls" turns her into "their beast, their thing" (p. 173). Filled with a mixture of pity and guilt, the narrator addresses the girl: "You are ill: no one heals you or caresses you softly. … How you must hate us, poor little girl!" (p. 175).

Brief and impressionistic, this *crónica* nevertheless holds hidden depths. To begin with, despite its seeming specificity, the character of the little girl-acrobat is not necessarily based on a "real" person. As Carolyn Steedman shows in *Strange Dislocations: Childhood and the Idea of Human Interiority, 1780–1930* (1995), the image of the orphaned girl-child, associated with acrobats and the circus, recurs like a leitmotiv throughout Western literature and culture during the nineteenth and twentieth centuries.[8] Steedman locates its origin in the character of Mignon in Goethe's *Wilhelm Meisters Lehrjahre* (Wilhelm Meister's Years of Apprenticepship, 1795–96), and argues that the long-lasting cultural life span of the figure of the deformed and helpless child acrobat is associated with the development of the modern concept of interiority and psychical self-awareness (Steedman, pp. 3–5).

Certainly, Nájera's girl-acrobat could be seen as a portrait of Nájera's "inner self" in which he presents himself, in the manner of the Decadent poets, as the artist who is misunderstood and mistreated by the masses, by society. It is interesting to note that in one of his best known poems, "Mis enlutadas" (My Women in Mourning), Nájera explicitly presents himself as a passive and victimized being, to the point of comparing himself with

[8] Carolyn Steedman, *Strange Dislocations: Childhood and the Idea of Human Interiority, 1780–1930* (London: Virago Press, 1995).

"the helpless martyred girl-child/ [who] bites the harpy/ who mistreats her."[9] Furthermore, among the nearly thirty pseudonyms Nájera used in his journalistic career at least one, "Crysantema," was feminine.[10]

The *crónica*'s title derives from an epithet the narrator applies to the girl-acrobat, "daughter of the air," which might at first seem an appropriate metaphor for a girl who flies on the trapeze. It could even be regarded as an uplifting metaphor (so to speak), one that poeticizes and gives some dignity to the harsh reality of an exploited child. Nevertheless, for Hispanists (as well as cultured Spanish American readers), Nájera's title immediately evokes the homonymous play of the Spanish golden age by Pedro Calderón de la Barca, written around 1653.[11] Calderón's play deals with the legend of Queen Semiramis of Babylon, who was saved by birds from perishing after her mother died in childbirth, hence her epithet "the daughter of the air." An orphan like the girl-acrobat, Semiramis grows up to become a woman of seductive beauty but ambitious and destructive passions. Semiramis is a baroque prototype of the nineteenth-century *femme fatale*, and she prefigures what the little girl-acrobat may well grow up to become.

If the girl-acrobat is an *alter ego*, of sorts, of Nájera himself, the ambiguity implicit in her epithet "daughter of the air" points to a similar ambivalence in Nájera himself as an author. Is the "daughter of the air" merely the helpess girl-child (like Goethe's Mignon) or is she also the tyrannical, man-devouring seductress Semiramis? Similarly, is Manuel Gutiérrez Nájera merely a kindly journalistic Proteus who pliantly molds himself to every circumstance, or is he a sadistic exploiter of children in his *crónicas* and stories? It is shocking to realize how many children die in Nájera's stories, from "La familia Estrada" (The Estrada Family) and "La balada de Año Nuevo" (The New Year's Ballad) to "La mañana de San Juan" (The Morning of San Juan) and "La pasión de Pasionaria" (The Passion

9 José Olivio Jiménez, *Antología crítica de la poesía modernista hispanoamericana* (Madrid: Hiperión, 1985), p. 109.

10 Gutiérrez Nájera, Margarita, *Reflejo: Biografía anecdótica de Manuel Gutiérrez Nájera* (Mexico: Instituto Nacional de Bellas Artes, 1960), p. 37.

11 Pedro Calderón de la Barca, *La hija del aire*, ed. Gwynne Edwards (London: Tamesis Books, 1970). Calderón was, along with Shakespeare and Molière, one of Nájera's idols. Besides his frequent allusions to *La vida es sueño* (Life is a Dream), one also finds in Nájera's collected theatre *crónicas* allusions to other plays by the Spanish Baroque master, such as *La devoción de la cruz* and *El médico de su honra*. In his article "El centenario de Calderón" (1881), Nájera complains bitterly about the lack of any commemoration of the tricentennial of Calderón's death in Mexico. See Manuel Gutiérrez Nájera, *Obras*, IV. *Crónicas y artículos sobre teatro, II (1881–1882)*, ed. Yolanda Bache Cortés and Ana Elena Díaz Alejo (Mexico: Universidad Nacional Autónoma de México, 1984), pp. 114–15.

of Pasionaria; *Cuentos completos*, pp. 115–23, 162–6, 195–9, 200–4). The following witticism from Nájera's story "La odisea de Madame Théo" (Madame Théo's Oddyssey, 1883) takes on ominous resonances after one has read "La hija del aire": "It is a mistake to believe that little girls who die without being baptized go to Limbo: little girls are never innocent when they die" (p. 233). As this text by Nájera demonstrates, the *modernistas*' subjectivism does not always lead to egotism. Nájera contemplates himself in the mirror of his writing, but he does not necessarily like what he sees. Despite its overt theme of social protest, Nájera's *crónica* also contains a profound and unsettling ethical reflection on his inner self and on his possible complicity, as a writer and intellectual, with the social evils he is denouncing. Nevertheless, the fact that this insight is reached by means of a dreamlike fantasy underscores the importance of the inner self to Nájera's writing, however dubious the self's ethical position may be.

José Martí, who gave the *crónica modernista* a wider international difusion and greater intellectual depth, dealt with the issue of subjectivity in a dramatically different way: by adopting in many of his chronicles a sort of pseudo-objective "God's eye view" of events not unlike that of French novelist Gustave Flaubert.[12] Martí sometimes inserted himself into his chronicles as a sort of eyewitness, but even then he used the third person, referring to himself in a curiously disparaging fashion as "a certain outcast," "a stranger," or "an insect." Nevertheless, Martí's *crónicas* are almost totally infused with his personal ideas about history, society, and culture. Like his speeches (he was one of the most charismatic and powerful orators of his time), his *crónicas* abound in aphorisms and maxims, such as "Man is nothing in himself, and what he is, is the product of his people"; "Everything that exists is a symbol"; "Art is a form of respect." Despite the occasional attempts by some Spanish American editors to censor his political views, Martí was able to turn even the most informative of his *crónicas*

[12] Flaubert's celebrated statement of authorial impersonality comes from his letter to Louise Colet dated December 9, 1852, and it reads in full: "An author in his book must be like God in the universe, present everywhere and visible nowhere. Art being a second Nature, the creator of that nature must behave similarly. In all its atoms, in all its aspects, let there be sensed a hidden, infinite impassivity. The effect for the spectator must be a kind of amazement. 'How is all that done?' one must ask; and one must feel overwhelmed without knowing why. Greek art followed that principle, and to achieve its effects more quickly, it chose characters in exceptional conditions – kings, gods, demigods. You were not encouraged to identify with the dramatis personae: the *divine* was the dramatist's goal." Gustave Flaubert, *The Letters of Gustave Flaubert (1830–1857)*, ed. Francis Steegmuller (Cambridge, MA: Harvard University Press, 1980), pp. 173–4. See also Gustave Flaubert, *Correspondance*, ed. Jean Bruneau (Paris: Gallimard, Bibliothèque de la Pléiade, 1973), II, p. 204.

into a highly personal text, written in a style that could not be mistaken for anyone else's. Domingo Faustino Sarmiento's comment to Paul Groussac in 1887 attests to Martí's success in this regard: "There is nothing in the Spanish language like Martí's bellowing, and, aside from Victor Hugo, France has not produced a writer of such metallic resonance."[13]

From New York City, where he lived for much of the latter part of his life, Martí sent his *crónicas* to prominent Spanish American newspapers like *La Opinión Nacional* in Caracas and *La Nación* in Buenos Aires. These *crónicas*, in turn, were widely reprinted throughout the continent. Martí also founded the newspaper *Patria* during the 1890s to further the cause of Cuban independence.

Martí's *crónicas* may be classified into three general types: the artistic and literary, the reportorial, and the "domestic." This latter type encompasses the texts Martí wrote for the section titled "En Casa" (At Home) of his newspaper *Patria*, in which he describes, in the same lyrical yet familiar style found in his letters, the modest social and political activities of the Cuban émigré communities in New York, Tampa, and Key West. In contrast, the artistic and literary *crónicas*, published in such diverse journals and dailies as *La Nación*, *El Partido Liberal* (Mexico), and the *Revista Venezolana*, have a lush descriptive style that has often been regarded as the epitome of the "artistic prose" of the *modernistas*.

However, it is in the reportorial chronicles that Martí uses the widest range of stylistic and rhetorical devices. Published mainly during the 1880s, these *crónicas* comprise the previously mentioned "Escenas europeas" and "Escenas norteamericanas." Their reportorial nature arises from the fact that they deal with the sort of events usually covered by reporters: political controversies, economic news, crime stories, disasters, etc. Nevertheless, Martí was less a reporter than a "foreign correspondent" and only rarely, such as at the inauguration of the Statue of Liberty in New York in 1886, did he chronicle an event that he had actually witnessed. His *crónicas* were in fact news summaries, gleaned mostly from North American and European newspapers. Martí's method in composing his *crónicas* was quasi-philological: taking advantage of New York's burgeoning press, he bought copies of the major dailies and systematically compared their coverage of the same event, preparing a composite narrative in a style so lively and descriptive that it seemed a firsthand account.[14] "Decirlo es verlo" (To say

[13] Cited by Manuel Pedro González and Ivan A. Schulman in José Martí, *Esquema ideológico* (Mexico: Editorial Cultura, 1961), p. 63.

[14] Andrés Iduarte, *Martí, escritor* (Havana: Ministerio de Educación, Dirección de Cultura, 1951), p. 140.

it is to see it), a phrase Martí used in his well-known *crónica* about the Charleston earthquake of 1886, summarizes his constant attempt to create an impression of immediacy through the evocation of the spoken word.

Martí's "Escenas," which were published weekly or fortnightly, posed an enormous challenge to his capacity as a writer, since he was required not only to enumerate and relate the week's events but also to comment on them within a coherent stylistic and ideological framework while keeping his discourse as impersonal as possible. It has frequently been remarked that Martí's "Escenas norteamericanas" have an epic scope, richness of descriptive detail, and vividness of characterization and description that gives them an almost novelistic character in the mold of the vast nineteenth-century novels like those of Balzac, Flaubert, Émile Zola, or Benito Pérez Galdós (1843–1920). However, unlike Flaubert, whose highly ironic depiction of reality intended to suggest that reality was ultimately impossible to fully understand, Martí's *crónicas* presupposed an underlying order to the often chaotic events being described. The teeming masses of New York, the colonizers of the West, the great statesmen and orators, the criminals, the intellectuals, the civic celebrations, the public controversies, the disasters – fires, earthquakes, railroad accidents – all the myriad characters and events of life in the United States and Europe that parade through Martí's *crónicas*, are seen as part of a single, coherent historical process.

A good example of Martí's struggle to achieve a unified journalistic vision is his 1889 *crónica* "Cómo se crea un pueblo nuevo en los Estados Unidos," whose title, owing to the double meaning of the Spanish word "pueblo" ("town" but also "people"), can be read either as "How a New Town is Created in the United States" or "How a New People is Created in the United States." In fact, the *crónica* allows for a more limited reading as a quasi-documentary account of a land rush in Oklahoma, and for a broader symbolic meditation on the national character of the United States.

Martí begins his *crónica* with two long paragraphs that start with almost the same sentence: "Todo lo olvidó Nueva York en un instante" (Everything was forgotten by New York in an instant) in the first paragraph, and "Todo lo olvida Nueva York en un instante" (Everything is forgotten by New York in an instant).[15] The word "everything" allows Martí, in the first paragraph, to summarize some of the major and minor events of that week in a series of rhetorical questions that fulfill the function of headlines:

> Everything was forgotten by new York in an instant. Did the Postmaster General die as much from illness as from sadness because his

[15] José Martí, *Letras fieras* (Havana: Letras Cubanas, 1985), pp. 301, 302.

> own Republican party took away from him the job he won bit by bit, from the cap to the chair, to give it instead to a long-bearded vote-getter who spends his time paying for rounds of beer and making friends with the neighborhood men? Does City Hall refuse to extend the lines of the elevated railroad that blemish the city and fill it with smoke and fright? Has a new national *cravat* become fashionable, with the three colors of the flag and the ends raised stiffly to the shoulders? (Martí, p. 301)

In the second paragraph, however, a present-tense variation of the first sentence introduces Martí's impressionistic account of a fire in New York's central railroad depot. Carefully composed in short, vivid sentences, this segment abounds in pictorial images, ironic asides, and artistic allusions to the light and colors of the fire:

> A fire worthy of the Centennial [of the United States' independence] consumes the grain depots of the central railroad. The river flows uselessly at its feet. The pumps, defeated, bellow and throw sparks. Six city blocks burn, and the flames – blackish, ruby red, yellow, russet – snap at each other, clasp each other, rise like waterspouts or whirlpools inside the shells of the walls like a storm on the Sun. The light shines for miles and glows upon the church steeples, paints a sharp lacework of shadows on the pavement, and falls on the façade of a school upon the sign that reads: "Girls." Mutely, the crowd of fifty thousand spectators watches the sea of fire boil with Roman-like emotions. (Martí, p. 302)

After the shocking images of the fire, Martí balances his *crónica* with a picturesque account of New Yorkers taking their Easter Sunday promenades along Fifth and Sixth Avenues. Here, he places special emphasis, as he does in his chronicle of the 1886 Charleston earthquake, on "los negros," the blacks of New York City, the sight of whom, in Martí's words, "gladdens the heart" (p. 303). Ever mindful of Cuban politics, and of the recent abolition of slavery in Cuba, Martí presents to his Spanish American readers the example of the "thousands of prosperous blacks who live in the neighborhoods of Sixth Avenue" who "love without fear; raise families and fortunes; debate and publish; change their physical type with the change in their souls" (p. 303).

Following this idyllic image of polished urbanity, however, the *crónica* moves to its main topic, the description of the Oklahoma Land Rush of 1889, an event that one urban specialist calls "one of the most bizarre and chaotic episodes of town founding in world history."[16] Images of simultaneity and speed as well as chaotic enumerations, irony, and an implicit moral condemnation predominate in this section of the *crónica*:

> And at that same hour, in the deserted plains, the eager colonists of the indian lands, awaiting the noon hour on Monday to invade the new Canaan, the ancient home of the poor Seminoles, the land of milk and honey, pray or raise a hubbub, and in that live frontier held only by the vigilant troops nothing else is heard but the shouted greeting of the former wretch turned property-owner, the speculator who sees foaming gold, or the rogue who profits from vice and death (Martí, pp. 303–4)

In this spectacle of thousands of people vying to claim a piece of land taken from the Indians, Martí clearly sees a warning to his fellow Spanish Americans about the expansionist designs of the United States, although, unlike his later and more celebrated essay "Nuestra América" (Our America, 1891), he avoids saying so explicitly. Instead, he focuses on the violence, the injustice, and the brute force being used to claim the Oklahoma lands, as well as on those aspects his Spanish American readers would find extremely bizarre, such as the various "women who have come alone, like the men, to 'take land' for themselves, or to speculate with those they buy from others," like Polly Young, "the lovely widow, who already did the same in Kansas," Nelly Bruce, "who lived in the forest," or Nanitta Daisy, "who knows Latin and has won two medals as a sharpshooter" (Martí, p. 307). Although Martí favored greater educational opportunities for women, like other Spanish American males of his time he still restricted females to the domestic sphere and often expressed his dismay at the freer behavior he saw in US women.

As was said earlier, Martí's success in infusing his *crónicas* with his subjectivity arises, paradoxically, from his avoidance of direct allusions to himself even as he exercises through his command of oratory and rhetoric a high degree of control over his representation of reality. As the title "Escenas norteamericanas" suggests, events in Martí's chronicles are usually described as a sequence of tableaux or scenes, not unlike the dioramas that were so popular in the Parisian arcades of the mid-nineteenth century – in which each immobile scene was brought to life by the voice and presence of an orator – or like a museum, in which disparate exhibits

16 John W. Reps, introduction to William Willard Howard's "The Rush to Oklahoma," http://www.library.cornell.edu/Reps/DOCS/landrush.htm (document accessed 8/4/05).

are linked together by the organizing discourse of the guide. For his Spanish American readers, Martí became a trusted guide who explained and brought to life their fragmentary glimpses of a foreign land.

As has been seen thus far, Nájera cannily brought fiction and imagination into the *crónica*, reducing its informative function to a bare minimum. On the other hand, Martí's powerful personality and political commitment allowed him to work more closely with the *crónicas*' reportorial aspects, turning them into vehicles for his own historico-political reflections.[17] Martí's fellow countryman Julián del Casal, however, displays a very different attitude in his *crónicas*, one that radically rejects journalism in favor of "Art for Art's Sake."

Unlike Nájera and Martí, Casal never wrote memorably in his *crónicas* about catastrophes or large-scale events such as earthquakes or wars. (He only wrote three short and highly elliptical pieces, as if to fulfill an obligation, in the daily *La Discusión*, about a fire in Havana on 17 May, 1890.)[18] Casal clearly had no room in his writing for such happenings, since his writing is rigorously introspective and personal: he wrote fully from the perspective of the "interior," to which I alluded with regard to Nájera. Ten years younger than Martí and four years younger than Nájera, Casal fully subscribed to the metaphor of literature as an interior, which was dear to the European Decadents. Thus, he wrote disparagingly about nature and the Cuban landscape in his well-known poem "En el campo" (In the Countryside):

> My languid senses less enchants
> the smell of a mahogany plant
> than a bedroom's sickly scent.[19]

For the Decadent, the metaphor of the interior signified their desire to turn literature into a more self-reflexive endeavor as a defensive response to the challenge posed by scientific discourse at the end of the nineteenth century. The interior – whether library, bedroom, or office – was seen as the

17 In a letter to Bartolomé Mitre y Vedia, Martí explains: "One of my defects is that I can not create things in bits and pieces. Instead, I want to fill small vessels with substance, and write newspaper articles as if they were books. Which is why I write calmly and with my true style only when I feel I am writing for people who will love me, and only when I am able, in brief successive works, to discreetly give shape on the outside to the inner work that already exists within my mind," *Obras completas*, IX (Havana: Editorial Nacional de Cuba, 1965), p. 16.

18 Julián del Casal, *Prosas*, pp. 138, 159–61.

19 Julián del Casal, *Poesías* (Havana: Consejo Nacional de Cultura, 1963), p. 190.

last refuge of art, eroticism, and play. It was the place where the Romantics' formerly powerful self, now turned more intimate, left behind the ambition to fuse Man and Nature in a harmonious whole, and was content with surrounding itself with a "second Nature" of man-made objects with which it could while away its exile from the world.

Decadence, it should be remembered, was regarded by its followers as an almost inevitable fate. After all, the physical sciences, following the thermodynamic concept of entropy (the tendency towards increasing randomness in orderly systems), claimed that the world would grow ever colder as it aged, and social thinkers such as Henry and Brooks Adams wrote about the unstoppable decadence of "civilized" societies.[20] Furthermore, as others reasoned, if society was "decadent" this also implied that it was "sick" (this was a favorite metaphor of Naturalist writers like Zola). As Susan Sontag points out, the use of illness as a metaphor for social injustice in modern political rhetoric harks back to the French Revolution, but it is in the second half of the nineteenth century when ideas such as "decadence" and "sickness" are firmly joined together when talking about society and culture.[21] The Decadent interior, besides being an office, library, or bedroom, could also be a hospital, and the artist could be thought of as a sick, bedridden individual, suffering from boredom or *spleen*. In the words of the French poet Charles Baudelaire (1821–67) in his *Petits poèmes en prose* (Little Prose Poems, 1869): "This life is a hospital where every patient is possessed by the desire to switch beds."[22]

While for others Decadence may have been a pose, for Casal, who suffered from tuberculosis during the last three years of his life, it was a sincere expression of his condition and his worldview. Although his previously cited diatribe against journalism was right in seeing journalistic discourse as inimical to self-expression and to an aestheticist view of writing, it also reflected Casal's own Decadentist attitude, which led him to reject nearly everything not associated with art and beauty. Needless to say, this attitude tended to discourage Casal from any attempt (like Nájera's and Martí's) to stamp his personality on his *crónicas*. Even so,

20 Brooks Adams, *The Law of Civilization and Decay: An Essay on History* (New York: Macmillan, 1895); and Henry Adams, *The Tendency of History* (Washington: Government Printing Office, 1896).

21 Susan Sontag, *Illness as Metaphor* (New York: Vintage Books, 1979), p. 78. One of the best commentaries on the topic of "illness" in post-romantic literature, and particularly in Decadence, is still Gian-Paolo Biasin, *Literary Diseases: Theme and Metaphor in the Italian Novel* (Austin: University of Texas Press, 1975), pp. 3–35.

22 Charles Baudelaire, *Petits poèmes en prose*, in *Oeuvres complètes de Charles Baudelaire* (Paris: Conard, 1926), p. 165.

the fourteen *crónicas* he published in the Havana daily *El País* during the late 1880s under the title "Crónica semanal" (Weekly Chronicle) attest to his desultory struggle with the journalistic side of the *crónicas*. In terms of their structure, for example, Casal's *crónicas*, like some of Nájera's, are thematically heterogeneous and fragmentary, composed of different sections dealing with events whose only connection was that of having occurred during the same week. Casal often inserted one or two of his own poems in the midst of his *crónica*, which neither Nájera nor Martí ever did, but this was probably tolerated by his editors because he was such a notable poet and also because his *crónicas* were addressed to a mostly feminine readership. Nevertheless, some of these *crónicas* do display a considerable unity of tone, and there are a few in which the various themes coincide and the *crónica* achieves a fragile coherence.

This is the case with the "Crónica semanal II" (the lack of a more poetic title is in itself telling). Illness and death comprise the unifying leitmotiv of this text in which, nevertheless, flashes of ironic humor are also present. Casal begins by informing us that during the past week (which, in his words, "has just given up the ghost"), the society of Havana has been, quite literally, a sick society, since almost everyone was suffering from the cold (Casal uses the French term *grippe*):

> Each house was turned into a hospital where the patients, if not in danger of dying, were nevertheless tormented by the rigors of this overwhelming illness whose march science does not know how to stop. The victims of *grippe* (such is the name of the illness) must resign themselves to withstand all kinds of tortures, from the fever that dulls the intelligence to the catarrh that places a humid veil before all objects. (Casal, *Prosas*, p. 16)

Casal personifies the illness with traits reminiscent of the topic of the femme fatale: "The *grippe* resembles those women of a certain age who, with tears in their eyes and their soul burning with love, throw themselves at the feet of young men obstinately asking for their love" (p. 16). This *femme fatale* "has good taste," Casal notes, "because it only visits civilized countries. Last year it was in Europe, now it has come to America" (p. 16).

As an epidemic, however, the *grippe* is far from being a catastrophe: "its caresses, if unpleasant, are harmless up to a point," says Casal (p. 16). Even so, he adds, "one must not be kind towards her. ... Her visit to this country is an act of refined cruelty" (p. 16). The *grippe* is, like Casal's own tuberculosis, a disease of civilization. Like tuberculosis, it is a disease that disintegrates, an illness of liquids and fever. It is, however, not fatal in the tropics, although it weakens the body and makes it return to a primitive, degenerate state: "Under the weight of this epidemic, even the most beautiful woman appears stained by ugliness; the most delightful book seems insipid; our closest friend seems perfidious, and our thought sinks into a lethargy like that of the beasts" (p. 16). As Casal portrays it, the *grippe* is an entropic, degenerating disease, although it would seem too undignified to be "decadent."

From this description of the *grippe*, Casal goes on to comment on "the unexpected suicide of a Mexican gentleman whose acquaintance I had the honor of making while he lived in this city" (p. 17). This mysterious individual seems to have been virtually an incarnation of a Decadentist character in the style of Des Esseintes in Joris-Karl Huysman's novel *À rebour*, and Casal's admiration for him is evident: "Whoever has sometime seen, in the theaters or in the boulevards, the heroic man who has deprived himself of his life so as not to lose his dignity, will keep in their memory the remembrance of that beautiful manly figure in whom could be seen the most sober elegance and a distinction beyond reproach" (p. 17). To complete his description of this turn-of-the-century prototype, Casal adds that he "preferred the contemporary poets whose compositions reflect the most delicate shadings of the modern soul, especially Baudelaire and Mallarmé" (p. 17). Perhaps it would not be too much to say that if this man had not existed, Casal would have had to invent him, since his story fits perfectly with the mood of this *crónica* and with Casal's disquisition on "end of the century melancholy" in the latter part of the text.

Nevertheless, perhaps the truly fictional character in this *crónica* is the no less mysterious "unknown lady" who wrote to Casal, according to him, to ask him about the meaning of the phrase "end of the century melancholy" (*tristeza fin de siglo*; *Prosas*, p. 18). Whether real or not, the "lady" serves Casal as a pretext, immediately following his presentation of the Decadent prototype of the "Mexican gentleman," to allude to his own meditations about the concept of decadence: "Save ours, no other end of the century has witnessed so many contradictory and unexpected things. Thus an uncertainty has arisen in many minds that grows more alarming every day. Our analysis has led us to understand that, after so many centuries, it is not possible to determine precisely how much humanity has progressed" (p. 18). The feeling of "decadence," notes Casal, is rooted in the sense of indeterminacy produced by entropy. A "sick" society has been drifting towards increased disorder, it has begun to dissolve and to be consumed, like a person afflicted with the *grippe* or with tuberculosis, and it is no longer possible to know which way "the arrow of time" (Sir Arthur Eddington's metaphor for entropy) is moving.[23] Civilization as a whole is for Casal like an immense hospital full of plague victims: "Knowing that this state of affairs can not go on forever because it makes our lives unbearable, some believe vaguely that a remedy will be discovered in the remaining decade of this century; but since there is also a fear that the hungry masses will cause a great social cataclysm, the uncertainty of which I have spoken, that is, the end of the century melancholy, is entering, like the microbes of an epidemic, into everyone's spirit, not only in Europe but also in all civilized countries" (p. 18).

Casal's *crónica* ends with two disparate segments: immediately following his somber meditations on decadence, he inserts one of his poems, "Vespertino" (Evening), later collected in his book *Nieve*, which also repeats the theme of death in its description of a sunset:

> Light is in agony. Over the green
> mountains rising over grey haze
> the evening star twinkles
> like the pupil of a dying virgin
> in her final hour ...
> The wave bemoans
> The Sun's death and falls asleep
> casting its sad cries to the wind. (*Prosas*, p. 19)

The *crónica*'s final section, however, is indicative of how Casal cared little, in the end, for the coherence of his chronicles. Here he comments, as if fulfilling a painful obligation, on two plays that were presented in Havana the previous week (pp. 19–20).

Casal's self-questioning Decadentist *crónicas* anticipate in some respects the tone of uncertainty that predominates in the *crónicas* of the younger generation of *modernistas* such as Rubén Darío, José Enrique Rodó, and Enrique Gómez Carrillo. But the *crónicas* by the "second wave" of *modernistas* also overtly display a tendency towards self-criticism couched in explicitly autobiographical elements; no longer do the *modernistas* hide their self in their *crónicas* for strategic reasons, like Martí, or mask it with fictions, like Nájera. Neither do they adopt Casal's somewhat defeatist attitude towards journalism. Instead, they speak openly about themselves, about their joys and pleasures, their worries and their

23 David Layzer, "The Arrow of Time," *Scientific American*, 6 (1975), pp. 59–60.

fears, as well as about their sometimes conflictive relationship with the world around them. Fully aware of their celebrity and of the sociopolitical responsibilities that came with it, the later *modernistas* realized that, in order to be modern, they needed to embrace change, and in order to remain relevant, they needed to reach out to their readers. Modifying the elitist attitude he had shown in the prologue to his first book of poems, *Prosas profanas* in 1896, Rubén Darío declared in 1905 in the preface to *Cantos de vida y esperanza*: "I am not a poet for the masses, but I know that I must inevitably go towards them."[24]

The writer's relation to society and to the world at large is one of the main overarching themes of these new *crónicas modernistas*. Encouraged by their cosmopolitan attitude and by their own increasingly frequent travels through the Americas, Europe, and the Orient, the *modernistas* turned many of their new *crónicas* into travel chronicles. It could be argued, of course, that Martí's "Escenas" were also a form of travel writing, but what is different in the new *crónicas* by Darío, Rodó, and Gómez Carrillo, among others, is their self-reflexive commentary on the experience of travel itself and how travel affects the writer's consciousness.

As was said in Chapter 1, after the deaths of Nájera and Martí, Darío, who was in many ways their literary heir, became the undisputed leader of *modernismo*. Nowhere is his debt to those earlier writers more evident than in his chronicles. Published and reprinted in Spanish and Spanish American journals and dailies, they were collected in books such as *Los raros* (The Strange Ones, 1896), *España contemporánea* (Contemporary Spain, 1901), *Peregrinaciones* (Pilgrimages, 1901), *La caravana pasa* (The Caravan Passes, 1903), *Tierras solares* (Lands of the Sun, 1904), and *El viaje a Nicaragua* (The Voyage to Nicaragua, 1909). Darío's chronicles, like Martí's, form a vast body of writings which can be divided into three basic types: the artistic and literary, the reportorial, and travel chronicles. Unlike the *crónicas* of Nájera and Martí, however, the quality of Darío's is very uneven; far too many (especially the reportorial chronicles) were hastily written occasional pieces. The books mentioned above, however, contain some of Darío's best prose.

Los raros offers the most significant examples of Darío's artistic and literary *crónicas*. These consisted of impressionistic profiles of past and present authors from Europe and Spanish America, selected mainly because of their marginality to their respective traditions. Most of the authors Darío chose to highlight in these *crónicas* were French; the majority were

[24] Rubén Darío, *Poesías completas* (Madrid: Aguilar, 1967), p. 753.

(and still remain) secondary figures, such as Jean Richepin, Rachilde, or Laurent Tailhade, but others, like Lautréamont, were later to be revered by the Avant-Garde. Among the non-French authors, Darío includes only two Spanish Americans, both Cubans: Augusto de Armas (1869–93) and José Martí. De Armas wrote in French and is a decidedly minor figure; Darío's chronicle on Martí, however, is important because it was one of the first literary evaluations written after Martí's death, and it served to call attention to Martí's stature as a founding figure of *modernismo*.

In his travel chronicles, which contain some of Darío's finest prose, the Nicaraguan poet develops a rhetorical strategy that attempts to reconcile the *modernistas*' quasi-philological reverence for past artistic and literary history with the modern imperative of almost-constant change. In one of his most famous autobiographical poems, "Yo soy aquel …" (I am that One …) in *Cantos de vida y esperanza*, Darío states that he had always wanted to be "*muy antiguo/ y muy moderno*" (very ancient and very modern; *Poesías completas*, p. 753). But, how can the poet's self – and the literature the self produces – embrace modernity and change without losing his identity? How can the poet reconcile the past (including his own past) with the present? Darío's "solution" to this conundrum, which was widely imitated by other *modernistas* of his generation, was to adopt the ancient literary and cultural topic of "conversion" (including its religious overtones). For Darío, the key to being modern while being true to himself was through the phenomenon of conversion, which Darío understood, in the Christian terms of St Paul, as the burial of the "old man" and the putting on of the new. Following the model set by St Augustine in his *Confessions* (AD 397), conversion in turn generates an impulse towards confession, that is, to tell the story of how the change in the self has occurred. In Darío's travel chronicles, the story he "confesses" as part of his conversion is presented as a "pilgrimage" (although the final destination is unclear); the poet sees himself as a pathetic wanderer – sometimes an exile, sometimes an expatriate – who is also a prisoner of his own celebrity.

In one of his best travel chronicles, *El viaje a Nicaragua*, Darío portrays his inner self as humble, weak, and in search of peace and happiness. Darío tries in this *crónica* to come to grips with his troubled personality and his celebrity (and the many responsibilities it entailed) in the context of the tale of his triumphant return to his native country in 1907. Read simply as a travel narrative, Darío's text describes the poet's itinerary from his departure from the French port of Le Havre until his arrival at the port of Corinto, in Nicaragua, after a brief stop in New York, and Darío's visits to the Nicaraguan cities of Masaya and León. Other segments of the book offer a brief cultural history of Nicaragua, covering aspects as diverse as the ethnic background of the Nicaraguan people, the origins and development of Nicaraguan literature, and the character traits of Nicaraguan women.

On a symbolic level, however, *El viaje a Nicaragua* is structured around an autobiographical and narrative voice that casts the tale of its return to its native land as a pilgrimage in search of peace, a return to the Origin, and a search for renewal. It is not surprising in this context that Darío "Orientalizes" Nicaragua in his descriptions, since, in the romantic philology Darío and the *modernistas* inherited, the Orient symbolized the origin of human civilization and a source of spiritual and cultural renewal. In an Orientalist frenzy, Darío compares Nicaraguan soldiers to those of Japan's Mikado, and the city of Masaya to Baghdad.[25] Nicaragua's prime export crop, coffee, grown amid volcanic mountains, symbolizes for Darío the capacity of Nicaraguan nature to reinvigorate his debilitated poetic powers: "One good cup of that black drink, well prepared, contains as many problems and poems as a bottle of ink" (*El viaje a Nicaragua*, p. 1039).

The possibilities of the *crónica* as a literary genre, as well as – it must be said – the monetary inducements offered by the journalistic profession, even attracted *modernista* writers such as José Enrique Rodó, whose inclinations were much more scholarly and reflective. In 1916, the popular Argentine magazine *Caras y Caretas* offered Rodó a paid trip to Europe if he would contribute a series of *crónicas* about the Old Continent.[26] Rodó accepted with alacrity; although at the age of 45 he was already well known and highly respected throughout Spanish America, he had never traveled far from his native Uruguay.

Of all the major *modernistas*, Rodó was the only one who was not a poet or a fiction writer: he was primarily an essayist and literary critic. Nevertheless, he too had begun his literary career in journalism; in 1895 he had founded the scholarly journal *Revista Nacional de Literatura y Ciencias Sociales* (National Review of Literature and Social Sciences). A few years later, becoming involved in politics, he began to collaborate on the daily *El Orden*. By 1907, he was publishing literary criticism and book reviews in the venerable Buenos Aires daily *La Nación*. In 1908 he was elected president of the Círculo de la Prensa (Journalists' Circle), and from 1912 through 1914 politics again led him to become involved in two daily news-

25 Rubén Darío, *El viaje a Nicaragua*, in *Obras completas* (Madrid: Afrodisio Aguado, 1950), pp. 1040, 1091.

26 Emir Rodríguez Monegal, "Introducción general" to José Enrique Rodó, *Obras completas* (Madrid: Aguilar, 1967), p. 59.

papers, *Diario del Plata* and *El Telégrafo* (Rodríguez Monegal, pp. 25, 28, 44, 48, 51 and 57). Like almost all other *modernistas*, however, his attitude towards journalism was ambivalent; in 1914 in a letter to a friend, Rodó acknowledged: "You know it well: journalism is not my vocation. But I have had to seek refuge in it, particularly since I stopped being a member of the Chamber of Deputies."[27]

The offer of a trip to Europe was irresistible. Rodó, who had already written in his book of essays *Motivos de Proteo* (Motives of Proteus, 1909) about the positive role of travel in the development of one's personality, and who, at least since 1904, ardently wished to visit Europe, did not miss his chance. He would go to Europe to "refresh the soul" – as he wrote to the Spaniard Miguel de Unamuno (1864–1936) – but, unbeknownst to him, he would also be putting to the test the "ethics of becoming" he had outlined in *Motivos de Proteo*. These were ideas similar to Darío's about how to reconcile modernity's demand for change with the desire to maintain a coherent image of the self.[28]

Travel to Europe was for Rodó, like Darío's return trip to Nicaragua, a pilgrimage to his origins and an attempt at self-renewal. Significantly, Rodó's primary destination in Europe, where he planned a lengthy stay, was Italy. Emir Rodríguez Monegal has pointed out that the example of Johann Wolfgang von Goethe may have influenced this decision, since Rodó writes in *Motivos de Proteo* about the key role Goethe's travels in Italy played in the German poet's artistic and intellectual development ("Introducción general," pp. 59–60). For Rodó, it seems, traveling to Italy meant not so much a return to Classical antiquity but rather a return to the romantic origins of philology, to the time when European consciousness so fruitfully focused its attention, as Rodó says in *Motivos de Proteo*, upon "the relics of sacred antiquity," upon "the buried marbles";[29] it was a return to the dawn of the nineteenth century, an age of great men (such as Goethe himself) who were also great egotists.

Unfortunately, Rodó's *crónicas* of his trip to Europe would also chronicle his journey towards death. Collected posthumously in 1918 under the title *El camino de Paros* (The Road to Paros), these *crónicas* were written in circumstances that are eerily evocative of the German author Thomas Mann's novel *Death in Venice* (1912), a work that Rodó never read. Like von Aschenbach, the protagonist of Mann's novel, Rodó finds in Italy the

[27] Cited in Rodríguez Monegal, p. 54.

[28] Cited in Rodríguez Monegal, p. 60.

[29] José Enrique Rodó, *Obras completas*, ed. Emir Rodríguez Monegal (Madrid: Aguilar, 1967), p. 422.

images of ideal beauty he had been seeking all his life, as he attests in his *crónica* titled "Y bien, formas divinas" (And Now, Divine Forms). Rodó's face-to-face encounter with the Classical ideal of beauty took place in the Ufizzi Gallery in Florence before a statue of Niobe, a mythical Greek queen who boasted of being a better mother than Leto, the mother of none other than the deities Apollo and Artemis. For her impiety, the gods killed Niobe's many children and she herself was turned into stone. Standing before this statue, which itself refers to a myth of petrification, Rodó reflects:

> And now, divine forms, ideas of marble, gods and godesses, demigods and heroes, nymphs and athletes, what else is necessary for you to achieve the fullness of being, a full and total reality? Why did a man who gloriously understood your beauty feel that from your motionless lips there came a melancholy nostalgia for consciousness and life? Wherefore Michaelangelo's hammer blow upon the brow of his Moses? But, why live, why change, when one has reached serene perfection? If life had carried you in its flow, time would have withered your youth, thought would have burned your serenity, passion would have stained your flesh, your beauty would have been but a fleeting shadow and today you would share death with the myriad human generations you have seen go by and dissolve, like the clouds of dust you have seen whirling around your pedestal.
>
> (*Obras completas*, p. 1274)

"Y bien, formas divinas" seemingly shows Rodó paralyzed before the unquestioned authority of "forms" received from antiquity; nevertheless, this *crónica* is more than just Rodó's homage to the *modernistas*' taste for ancient Greek and Roman culture. Its very writing attests to an instant of "conversion," to a sudden realization (even its title evokes abruptness and surprise). In this chronicle, Rodó suggests that he has understood how tightly linked writing and history are: the "divine forms" will always be apart from the world, "serene like the stars in the sky" (p. 1276), but the writing that attempts to copy them belongs to this world, and its worldly fate is to become a petrification, a shadowy fossil that attests to the passage of time.

Rodó's observations about time and writing in "Y bien, formas divinas" echo some of his earlier comments about journalistic writing in a 1914 article titled "Cómo ha de ser un diario" (What a Newspaper Must Be Like):

> Herbert Spencer's theory of style that we were all taught in school, which reduces the secret of good literary form to an economy of attention, is totally useless and false when one tries to understand the nature of artistic expression, but it defines well the ideal of form that is typical of journalism, in which the economy of attention and time is a goal that is naturally imposed by a type of reading that must be done in the midst of the urgencies of our daily work and with a clear awareness of the epehemeral condition of what one reads.
>
> Ever more closely identified with the complex life of society, but in a necessarily brief and changeable way, the Press must be like the shadow of society's body: true and faithful like the shadow, but also like a shadow, airy and fleeting. (*Obras completas*, p. 1201)

Despite this text's somewhat negative tone, the journalistic principles of "economy of attention and time" may be found also in Rodó's fragmentary essays in *Motivos de Proteo*. Further, Rodó's purpose, to turn *Motivos de Proteo* into an "open work," may also be seen as echoing journalism's ambition to be like "the shadow of society's body." During his trip to Italy, Rodó tried to learn, to become flexible and open to what was new; in another of his *crónicas*, "Recuerdos de Pisa" (Memories of Pisa), for example, he aludes to the Italian Avant-Garde artists: "Marinetti's Futurists, who clamor, as I have just read among the slogans in their newspaper, for the 'violent modernization of the past-loving city.' And certainly this city is one of those!" (*Obras completas*, p. 1268). Nevertheless, Rodó, who had greeted *modernismo* itself with some skepticism,[30] was unlikely to applaud an artistic movement that, even more than *modernismo*, made a fetish out of novelty. Like Mann's von Aschenbach, who, infatuated with the beautiful boy Tadzio, stays in Venice and perishes in a cholera epidemic, Rodó, who was already ill with a kidney infection, stayed on in Italy working on his writings, and died alone in the luxurious Hotel des Palmes in Palermo on May 1, 1917.[31]

Perhaps fittingly, the last great chronicler of the *modernista* age, the Guatemalan Enrique Gómez Carrillo, was a writer whose considerable celebrity in his day was founded almost exclusively on his work as a jour-

30 The first lines of Rodó's well-known review of Darío's second major book, *Prosas profanas*, expressed his nationalistic misgivings about *modernismo*'s cosmopolitan attitude: " 'He's not America's poet,' I once heard someone say when the flow of an animated literary talk stopped to consider the author of *Prosas profanas* and *Azul*. Those words had a reproachful tone, but although opinions differed about the judgment implied by that expression, there was unanimous assent for the negation itself. Undoubtedly, Rubén Darío is not America's poet" (*Obras completas*, p. 169).

31 Rodríguez Monegal, "Introducción general," pp. 66–8.

nalist. Paradoxically, it is due to this very fact that he has been all but forgotten today. Although he wrote a few novels, Gómez Carrillo was not a poet, and instead devoted his energies fully to journalism. A protégé of Darío, who gave him his first job in the Guatemalan newspaper *El Correo de la Tarde* in 1890,[32] Gómez Carrillo later moved to Madrid and finally settled in Paris, from where he devoted himself to conveying to his Spanish American readership the experience of France, and specifically of Paris, in all its aspects. As John W. Kronik points out:

> In an all-encompassing sweep, he [Gómez Carrillo] touched on every facet of French habits, from the Folies-Bergère to the patriotic impulse, from Parisian ladies' taste for the provocative black hose to Antoine's "Théâtre Libre." Generally, he registered his impressions of sights he had just witnessed, events that had just taken place, or people he had just met. He focused on matters of the day: recent plays, art expositions, books. His comments were not always laudatory (he did not, for instance, like the paintings of the Cubists, and he deplored the state of French criticism), but in any case his readers were enlightened by his articles, and more often than not they were subjected to the contagiousness of unabashed enthusiasm.[33]

Despite his frivolous pose, however, Gómez Carrillo was much more well-read and thoughtful than his chronicles sometimes suggested. As Max Henríquez Ureña has observed: "There is in his *crónicas* a vast amount of readings and knowledge that is mentioned without fanfare, almost in passing … he preferred to seem superficial rather than erudite or pedantic. … Many of his apparently superficial chronicles are in fact richly-documented essays that required a long and patient creation" (*Breve historia del modernismo*, pp. 393–4).

Another significant trait of Gómez Carrillo's *crónicas* is that virtually all of them are examples of travel writing. Just as journalism was for Gómez Carrillo the quintessentially modern way of writing, travel was for him a quintessentially modern way of life, which he embraced with gusto. His descriptions of life in Paris, as well as his travels to Greece, Egypt, and Japan, appeared in newspapers such as *La Nación* and *La Razón* in Buenos Aires, and *El Liberal* in Madrid, and were collected in books with titles such as: *De Marsella a Tokío* (From Marseille to Tokyo, 1906), *La Grecia*

32 Max Henríquez Ureña, *Breve historia del modernismo* (Mexico: Fondo de Cultura Económica, 1954), p. 390.

33 John W. Kronik, "Enrique Gómez Carrillo, Francophile Propagandist," *Symposium*, 21 (1967), pp. 51–2.

eterna (The Eternal Greece, 1906), and *La sonrisa de la esfinge: sensaciones de Egipto* (The Smile of the Sphinx: Sensations of Egypt, 1913).

One of his most striking *crónicas*, written in a reflective mood, is "La psicología del viaje" (The Psychology of Travel, 1919), in which he offers a critical meditation on the art of travel writing itself. Gómez Carrillo begins his text with the surprising prediction – in view of his fame as a travel writer – that traveling will soon be "bankrupt" as a form of "intellectual penetration and study" (in his words).[34] Paraphrasing the French psychologist Paul Bourget, he asks: "Why travel … since we will never be able to know the souls of the people of other countries? Why go to far-off places in search of human documents, when we are not even capable of deciphering the documents of our own homeland, our own family, our very being …? The Greek's *know thyself* is but a deceitful fantasy. We will never know ourselves, just as we will never know our fellow beings" (Gómez Carrillo, p. 8).

Gómez Carrillo's reflections on travel and travel writing spring from a deep skepticism towards the early twentieth-century *modernista* strategies of self-analysis and self-renewal (the triad of conversion, confession, and pilgrimage posited by Darío). Not only is the old romantic tradition of the "sentimental journey," of travel as a means of acquiring self-knowledge, useless, Gómez Carrillo points out, but travel itself has become unnecessary as a form of historical and philological inquiry, since there are already innumerable texts through which the researcher can more easily understand the *Volksgeist* of foreign countries. In view of these ideas, what is the function of the travel writer? Gómez Carrillo posits that the modern travel writer should simply aspire to transcribe the sights, smells, sounds, and experiences of the foreign lands he visits as they affect his consciousness. This he must do without attempting to give them a transcendental or psychologistic interpretation, or abandoning the harmonious and artistic style of modernist prose. The *modernista* travel writer, says Gómez Carrillo, should be a kind of *voyageur/voyeur*, or better yet, a sort of *medium* who receives and transmits the experiences of travel for the benefit of readers, who may never be able to travel, or if they do, will probably fall prey to the banal itineraries of the Baedeker or the *Guide Bleu*. For Gómez Carrillo, the *modernista* travel writer is the purveyor of a luxury product: a refined artistic reconstruction of unusual scenes and

[34] Enrique Gómez Carrillo, "La psicología del viaje," *El primer libro de las crónicas* (Madrid: Mundo Latino, 1919), p. 7.

sensations. Indeed, sensationalism, occasionally verging on pornography, is a common trait of many of Gómez Carrillo's travel chronicles.

"La psicología del viaje" is also valuable because it shows the Guatemalan chronicler's awareness of the corrosive effect of the new techniques of representation, such as photography and the cinema, on the nineteenth-century notions of literature and art. In a scene that prefigures Jorge Luis Borges's celebrated short story "The Aleph" (1949), Gómez Carrillo remembers his astonishment upon first coming across a book of photographs of foreign locales:

> How well I remember the first time I enjoyed the lightheadedness caused by that mysterious drug!
>
> It was in a Bank. I had stepped in to cash a check. Upon a table there lay a huge infolio with a title in English that meant something like "the Universe in your hand." ... There was not a line of text. Only photographs. Shots of all sorts of places, exotic vistas, strange and fantastic vistas. ... Between the branches of a tree-lined tropical avenue walked an elephant covered in silks. ... A rider rode across an immense desert of sand. ... A tower, a column, a gothic steeple. ... Then a narrow street full of people who were not like those I saw every day, a street so narrow it looked like a corridor, and in that corridor were the most garish rags, the richest hangings, the most violently clashing colors, and beneath that flight of multicolored wings, the people, the extraordinary people, wrapped in purple mantles. ... Then a lake covered in lateen sails. ... Later, a Babylon of steel, an inferno of trains, automobiles, rails, steel wires, masts, chimneys. ... I don't know! The entire Universe was there, between my hands. And I traveled through it, entranced. (Gómez Carrillo, pp. 27–8)

Photographs and movies not only make travel for the sake of knowledge and personal improvement superfluous for the ordinary individual, they also fulfill the desire for empirical accuracy that underlies much of nineteenth-century art and writing, thus posing a challenge for the *modernista* writer, who must satisfy the public's incessant craving for new sensations. While Gómez Carrillo was not himself an Avant-Gardist (he abhorred Cubism, for instance, as his chronicle "El cubismo" [1914] shows), he was clearly aware of the new forces that were rapidly undermining the foundations of art and life during the waning years of *la belle époque*, and that were opening new possibilities for artistic and literary creation.

With the death of Gómez Carrillo in 1927, the cycle of the *crónica modernista* came largely to an end. The *crónica*, which had come from

France to Spanish America, returned to France, but not without leaving its descendants. If it never achieved, in the opinion of many of its practitioners, the dignity of a full-fledged literary genre, it was enough, however, to guarantee its survival. Forged by the *modernistas*' uneasy collaboration with journalism, the *crónica* became, among other things, a stupendous vehicle for literary intercommunication and experimentation. In the *crónica*, the *modernistas* shared their ideas about literature, politics, and society, outlining concepts they would later develop more extensively in the genre of the essay. They also experimented with narrative themes and techniques, rehearsing materials they would develop into short stories and novels. And, of course, they explored in the *crónicas*' prose issues such as the role of subjectivity in art that they would treat time and again in their poetry. The *crónica* indeed deserves to be considered the cornerstone of the *modernistas*' house of literature.

Further Reading

Corona, Ignacio and Beth E. Jörgensen, eds., *The Contemporary Mexican Chronicle: Theoretical Perspectives on the Liminal Genre* (Albany: State University of New York Press, 2002). Despite the term "contemporary" in its title, this useful critical anthology centered on Mexico offers articles on *modernista* chroniclers such as Nájera, as well as on Avant-Garde authors such as Salvador Novo (1904–74) and more recent writers, ranging from Carlos Monsiváis (1938–) to Elena Poniatowska (1932–), Juan Villoro (1956–), and even Subcomandante Marcos (!).

González, Aníbal, *La crónica modernista hispanoamericana* (Madrid: José Porrúa Turanzas, 1983). The first book-length study of the *modernista* chronicles, offers detailed readings of *crónicas* by Martí, Nájera, Casal, Darío, Rodó, Gómez Carrillo, and discusses the *crónicas*' legacy in both *modernista* and contemporary Spanish American prose narrative.

Ramos, Julio, *Desencuentros de la modernidad en América Latina: literatura y política en el siglo XIX* (Mexico: Fondo de Cultura Económica, 2003). Focused mostly on the *modernistas*' political leanings and on their reaction to Spanish American modernization; chapters 4 and 5 of this book offer an extensive discussion of the *crónicas*, particularly as they reflect the *modernistas*' view of urban life.

Rotker, Susana, *The American Chronicles of José Martí: Journalism and Modernity in Spanish America* (Hanover, NH: Dartmouth Publishing Group, 2000). The best study by far of Martí's "Escenas Norteamericanas" and of his contribution to modern Spanish American journalism.

3

The *Modernista* Short Story

The *modernista* short story was one of the earliest and most successful by-products of the narrative experiments carried out by the *modernistas* within the brief confines of the *crónica*. Indeed, the *modernistas*' modernizing penchant focused almost as intensely on the short story genre as on poetry itself. Significantly, Rubén Darío's first great literary success was achieved with *Azul…* (1888), a collection of short stories accompanied by a handful of poems. Like Darío, the early *modernista* Manuel Gutiérrez Nájera, despite his prestige as a poet, also chose a short story collection as his first published work. *Cuentos frágiles* (1883) was Nájera's first and only book published during his lifetime, and it is also the first book of *modernista* short stories. Many of Nájera's stories in *Cuentos frágiles* (and in posthumously collected anthologies such as *Cuentos color de humo* [Stories the Color of Smoke], 1898) had their origin as journalistic chronicles, or parts of chronicles. Nájera often imbedded his fictions superficially in a journalistic context, from which they could be easily detached and collected as short stories; this is the case with tales such as "La novela del tranvía" (The Street-Car Novel), "La venganza de Mylord" (Mylord's Revenge), and "La hija del aire." Sometimes, however, the journalistic element is inseparable from the fictional narrative, as in "Los amores del cometa" (The Loves of the Comet), Nájera's fanciful description of the Great September Comet of 1882, or the dream-like "La odisea de Madame Théo" (Madame Théo's Oddyssey), whose protagonist is the real-life French singer Louise Théo.

Why this particular interest of the *modernistas* in the short story? As usual, there was a variety of reasons: to begin with, the *modernistas* gravitated towards whatever was perceived as new or modern, and the literary short story, despite its long and distinguished history harking back to the Middle Ages, had recently undergone a virtual reinvention in the work of Edgar Allan Poe. Poe did away in his stories with the didactic and moralizing elements of earlier tales, as well as with the picturesque description of manners that was common in much of Romantic narrative. Instead, he brought to the genre an emphasis on narrative intensity as well as on morbid psychology and bizarre occurrences. The *modernistas* were particularly interested in Poe's psychological approach to the short story, in his exploration of subjectivity. As Rubén Darío commented in his essay "Edgar Poe y los sueños" (Edgar Poe and Dreams, 1913):

> If Baudelaire created a new sensation, his master Poe unleashed veritable mental cataclisms and earthquakes. What is most marvelous about Poe's art – writes Bliss Perry, cited by Lauvrière – is that this embittered and lonely artist was capable, through the use of such deplorable materials as negations and abstractions, shadows and superstitions, disordered fantasies and dreams of physical horror, or strange crimes, of producing works of such imperishable beauty.[1]

An excessive sense of decorum and concern with poetic form precluded many *modernistas* from performing in their verse the deep personal introspection that the changing concept of literature at the turn of the century demanded. Instead, this function was fulfilled by the short story. Although some *modernista* short stories, such as those of Darío in *Azul…*, are little more than allegories of aesthetic theories (most notably, "El rey burgués" [The Bourgeois King] and "El pájaro azul" [The Blue Bird]), a great many are especially concerned with the role of the artist's inner life in his creative work. While the *crónicas*, despite the *modernistas*' efforts, were still nominally oriented towards the outside world of public events, the *modernista* short stories tried to go beyond surface appearances in order to probe the hidden motives of human conduct and of artistic creativity. The *modernistas*' psychological inquiry most often took an introspective form, in which the writer analyzed himself and delved into his consciousness, seeking out the underlying reasons for his literary vocation, the cause of his devotion to "the horror of literature" (as Darío stated in his poem "Cantos de vida y esperanza").

Modernismo's penchant for psychology was not derived solely from the Romantic and post-Romantic literary tradition of Poe and Baudelaire, of course, but was also nurtured by the increased scientific interest in mental life displayed in nineteenth-century culture. Although only late *modernistas* such as Leopoldo Lugones, Julio Herrera y Reissig, and the Venezuelan

[1] Rubén Darío, *El mundo de los sueños*, ed. Ángel Rama (Río Piedras: Editorial Universitaria, 1973), p. 194.

Manuel Díaz Rodríguez (1871–1938), were able to have some access to the ideas of Freudian psychoanalysis, earlier *modernistas* did share with Sigmund Freud many of the basic psychological concepts circulating in European culture at the turn of the nineteenth century. They were aware of the work of Jean-Martin Charcot (who was Freud's teacher), and had read popularizing books such as Hippolyte Taine's *De l'intelligence* (On Intelligence, 1871), Paul Bourget's *Essais de psychologie contemporaine* (Essays in Contemporary Psychology, 1883), and Maurice Barrès's *Trois stations de psychothérapie* (Three Stages of Psychotherapy, 1891). The concept of the unconscious itself, as has been pointed out:

> became very popular in all of Western Europe with the publication, in 1868, of Eduard von Hartmann's *Philosophy of the Unconscious*. In the 1870s, there were at least a half-dozen books with the word 'unconscious' in their titles. Freud certainly invented neither the term nor the concept(s) of the unconscious.[2]

During the same years when Freud was establishing the foundations of psychoanalysis in his study of dreams, neuroses, and drives, the *modernistas* were writing stories that focused insistently on dreams, fantasies, and aberrant behavior. Salient examples may be found among some of the most frequently anthologized *modernista* short stories, such as Nájera's "El sueño de Magda" (Magda's Dream, 1883), "La mañana de San Juan" (The Morning of Saint John's Day, 1883), and "Rip-Rip el aparecido" (Rip-Rip the Reappeared, 1890); Darío's numerous and scattered fantastic tales, such as "Thanatopia" (1893), "La pesadilla de Honorio" (Honorio's Nightmare, 1894), "La larva" (The Larva, 1910), and "Huitzilopoxtli (Leyenda mexicana)" (Huitzilopoxtli [Mexican Legend], 1915), Lugones's *Las fuerzas extrañas* (Strange Forces, 1906), the Mexican Amado Nervo's (1870–1919) *Cuentos misteriosos* (Mysterious Stories, 1920); and Díaz Rodríguez's *Confidencias de Psiquis* (Revelations of Psyche, 1897), "Las ovejas y las rosas del padre Serafín" (Father Serafín's Sheep and Roses), "Música bárbara" (Barbarous Music), and "Égloga de verano" (Summer Eclogue), all from 1922.

Nájera's *Cuentos frágiles*, as mentioned earlier, is the first book of *modernista* short stories ever published, and Nájera himself is regarded

2 "Unconscious," in *Critical Terms for Literary Study*, ed. Frank Lentricchia and Thomas McLaughlin (Chicago, University of Chicago Press, 1990), p. 148.

by critics as the first important *modernista* short story writer.[3] Before discussing a story from that book, however, it is worth taking a brief look at one of the many tales imbedded in his chronicles, one that was not collected in a book until long after Nájera's death: "El sueño de Magda" (its title was given by the critic E. K. Mapes, since it is imbedded in a series of chronicles by Nájera bearing the generic title "La vida en México" [Life in Mexico]).[4] This brief and enigmatic narrative almost seems to prefigure Surrealism in its evocation of the symbolic landscape of dreams. Magda is a woman who watches from her balcony as the rain falls in Mexico City. The third-person narrator tells of how this event evokes in Madga fearful memories of a nightmare she had the previous night. The nightmare, which consists of a vision of universal deluge, ends with Magda falling from the top of a stone cross onto a granite obelisk after having her eyes pierced by the beaks of owls. Nájera simply relates this dream, leaving possible interpretations to be developed by the reader. Interestingly, this story later became a chapter in Nájera's only known novel, *Por donde se sube al cielo* (discussed in Chapter 4 of this book). In its new context, the story becomes more clearly related to the issue of the artist's inner life, when Magda is revealed to be, in large measure, a female *alter ego* of the author himself.

"La mañana de San Juan," from *Cuentos frágiles*, is one of Nájera's most widely anthologized tales. Its plot is reminiscent of the sort of tragic event that is commonly reported in newspapers: two young brothers play with toy boats near a small dam on their parent's farm; the older one falls into the water; his younger sibling makes desperate attempts to save him, but they ultimately prove fruitless. In a highly symbolic scene, the drowning child manages to give his brother his small gold watch. Later, when the boys' mother, who had been ill and bedridden, kisses her dead son, she dies as well.

This harrowing event, which the narrator describes in heart-rending detail, is framed by a stylized poetic invocation of the morning of Saint John's Day. (The feast day of 24 June, honoring St John the Baptist, is traditionally linked to beauty, renewal, and fertility.) The feast day morning is personified as a beautiful maiden whose charms, sullied by contact with city life, are experienced in all their purity in the countryside: "Oh, little

3 See Enrique Pupo-Walker, "El cuento modernista: su evolución y características," in *Historia de la literatura hispanoamericana,* II. *Del neoclasicismo al modernismo*, ed. Luis Iñigo Madrigal (Madrid: Ediciones Cátedra, 1987), p. 517.

4 See Manuel Gutiérrez Nájera, *Cuentos completos*, ed. E. K. Mapes (Mexico: Fondo de Cultura Económica, 1987), p. 252n.

morning of Saint John's, you of the clean shirt and perfumed soaps, I wish I could regard you far from these cauldrons where humanity boils; I'd like to see you in the open air, where you still appear virginal, with your arms so white and your locks still wet!"[5] The story juxtaposes, in bitterly ironic contrast, the loveliness of the morning of Saint John's Day with the terrible tragedy that once happened on that very day. Its psychological impact emanates from this harsh juxtaposition, which strongly suggests that all great beauty, be it that of nature or of art, is ultimately cold and cruel. As the older brother drowns, the narrator underscores nature's sublime indifference in the face of human tragedy: "The stars began to come out in the sky. It seemed as if they were watching the tragedy of those three interlinked hands that didn't want to let go, and yet they let go! And the stars couldn't help them, because the stars are very cold and very high!"[6] Similarly, the ornate and elegant language in which Nájera tells this sad tale, along with the dying child's emblematic gold watch, points to an inhuman coldness at the heart of the *modernista* search for artistic perfection.

Like "El sueño de Magda," "Rip-Rip el aparecido," from *Cuentos color de humo*, is also narrated as a dream, although it begins in a more conventionally literary way as a gloss of Washington Irving's "Rip van Winkle" (which Nájera claims not to have read). Nájera's version, like Irving's legend, is the nightmarish tale of a man who gets drunk and falls asleep inside a cave, where he sleeps for many years. When he finally awakens, he is already old and is not recognized by his wife nor by his closest friends. In the end, Rip-Rip runs aways from the town, and only when he sees his reflection in a stream does he realize the cause of his predicament. Rip-Rip then commits suicide by drowning himself in the stream. This story may be interpreted as an allegory of personal identity, since the narrator tells us in the last lines of the story that Rip-Rip "was not one man, he was many men … perhaps all men."[7]

As a journalist who used over twenty different pseudonyms throughout his career, Nájera clearly had more than a purely aesthetic interest in the issue of the artist's personal identity. The story's theme of self-reflection and self-analysis (evocative of the myth of Narcissus) takes a surprising turn at the end, when the third-person narrator meditates on the writing of this story and its ultimate meaning:

5 Nájera, *Cuentos completos*, p. 195.
6 Nájera, *Cuentos completos*, p. 198.
7 Nájera, *Cuentos completos*, p. 283.

> Isn't this an extravagant dream? ... How long did [Rip] sleep? How much time is needed for those that we love and who love us to forget us? Is forgetting a crime? Are those who forget, evil? ... Jesus of Nazareth acted properly in bringing back to life only one man – one who had no wife, no children, and who had just died. It is good to heap a lot of earth upon corpses.[8]

Although reminiscent of Edgar Allan Poe, these lines also echo Nájera's anguished complaints about the impermanence of journalistic writing and the fickleness of readers, in the obituary he wrote for his friend, the journalist Alfredo Bablot:

> And all of that is lost! ... All that talent has been quenched like the "castle" that sent out such shining rockets into the air! Over there, in the anthologies where our thought is locked up as in a coffin! In the memory of friends that also dies out...! The journalist creates for oblivion! [9]

As Gabriela Mora has observed, Rubén Darío's fantastic tales, published mostly between 1893 and 1914, are written in a spare, economical style that is markedly different from the more ornate style featured in *Azul...* as well as in the stories of Nájera.[10] Although this stylistic difference may be due to the fact that Darío dashed these stories off hurriedly for publication in journals and newspapers such as *Caras y Caretas* (Buenos Aires), *La Nación* (Buenos Aires), *Mundial Magazine* (Paris), and *Diario de Centro-América* (Guatemala), the stories do reflect Darío's deep and abiding fascination with occult and hermetic themes, as well as his admiration for Poe's narrative art. It may also be argued that Darío's "fantastic" or "strange" short stories, like those of Leopoldo Lugones some years later, have a double thrust that is not only psychological but also concerned with issues of literary representation. Along with their exploration of extreme psychological conditions and strange occurrences, these stories also explore the limits of storytelling (in terms of the range of themes and events that could be incorporated into their narration) as well as the "strangeness," the artificiality, of the very act of telling a story itself.

[8] Nájera, *Cuentos completos*, pp. 283–4.

[9] Manuel Gutiérrez Nájera, *Obras: Crítica literaria, I*, ed. E. K. Mapes and Ernesto Mejía Sánchez (Mexico: Universidad Nacional Autónoma de México, 1959), p. 471.

[10] Gabriela Mora, *El cuento modernista hispanoamericano: Manuel Gutiérrez Nájera, Rubén Darío, Leopoldo Lugones, Manuel Díaz Rodríguez, Clemente Palma* (Lima–Berkeley, Latinoamericana Editores, 1996), p. 91.

Darío's "Thanathopia" is ostensibly a horror story about a British doctor and hypnotist who is married to a female vampire, but the story's first-person, confessional tone (it is narrated by the doctor's son) allows it to become, ambiguously, a fable about father–son relationships. The protagonist and narrator, James Leen, is an eccentric English professor and expatriate living in Buenos Aires who tells his story to a group of friends in a beer hall. Leen tells how, after his mother's death, his father, who never showed him affection, sent him off to study at a boarding school. The story's surprising ending is prefigured by certain enigmatic phrases spoken by the narrator, which Darío underlines, such as: "Physically, I was the veritable image of my mother (or so I have been told) *and I suppose that is why the doctor looked at me as little as possible*."[11] The explanation of this and other phrases is seen at the end, when the narrator is taken by his father to meet his stepmother, who turns out to be the corpse of his mother, kept in an "undead" state by the father's hypnotic arts.

"La pesadilla de Honorio," as its title indicates, is the description of a nightmare. Enrique Anderson Imbert has pointed out the story's sources in Thomas De Quincey's *Confessions of an English Opium Eater* (1821), and the narrator himself quotes in translation a fragment from De Quincey's book: "How and when did the following phrase by a dreamer appear in Honorio's memory: *the tyranny of the human face*?" (The original phrase from De Quincey reads: "That affection which I have called the tyranny of the human face.")[12] The nightmare in fact consists of an overwhelming vision of a multiplicity of human faces, which gradually turn into a series of masks that signify the seven deadly sins. In the final sentence, the narrator suggests that Honorio's hallucination or dream might have been simply the product of his drunken revelry at Carnival.

However, as in Nájera's "Rip-Rip el aparecido," identity is clearly at issue here, particularly in the *modernistas*' ever-present concern for the relation between writing and subjectivity. Following the antique belief, still prevalent at the turn of the nineteenth century, that the contours of the face and head revealed the individual's "inner self," Honorio, whose very name connotes "honesty," is a "reader" of human physiognomy. Nevertheless, instead of uncovering people's interiority, Honorio's "reading" leads him to see humanity as a grotesque spectacle, and the language of faces, after revealing only depravity and sin, turns into a "foreign" language, as

[11] Rubén Darío, *Cuentos fantásticos*, ed. José Olivio Jiménez (Madrid, Alianza Editorial, 1976), p. 33.

[12] See Enrique Anderson Imbert, *La originalidad de Rubén Darío* (Buenos Aires: Centro Editor de América Latina, 1967), p. 235.

the faces become a procession of enigmatic masks which, tellingly, are of Oriental origins.

Alcohol and drugs appear more prominently in "Huitzilopoxtli (Leyenda mexicana)." This late story (it was published in 1915, the year before Darío's death) may be seen as Darío's attempt to understand the significance of an event – the Mexican Revolution – which contributed to the demise of the *modernista* ideology and aesthetic. Darío views the Revolution as an act of mass immolation in the style of the Aztec sacrifices. The story's most satisfying aspect is its effective evocation of an atmosphere of mystery, fanaticism, and menace.

The first-person narrator, a journalist sent to cover the events of the Mexican Revolution, teams up with an American journalist with the amusing name of John Perhaps, and a bizarre Basque renegade priest turned colonel in the revolutionary army, named Reguera. On their way to one of Pancho Villa's encampments, the ex-priest insistently talks about how "the destiny of the Mexican nation is still in the hands of the primitive aboriginal deities."[13] The narrator-protagonist is intrigued, and asks Reguera to elaborate. Reguera argues that Francisco I. Madero's triumph over the dictatorship of Porfirio Díaz was due to his belief in spirits and specifically to his "contacts" with the ancient Aztec gods. While the narrator and Reguera talk and drink *comiteco* (a liquor made from fermented maize), the American journalist is lost from sight along the winding mountain road. Later, they come upon a group of insurgents but are not allowed to proceed, and must spend the night beneath some trees. Before going to sleep, the narrator and Reguera share some marihuana-laced cigarettes. A dreamlike scene then ensues in which the narrator, unable to sleep and hearing the howling of coyotes nearby, moves into the bush to investigate, with gun at the ready. After a while, he comes upon a grotesque scene: beneath an enormous Aztec stone idol, which the narrator recognizes as belonging to the goddess of death, a sacrifice is taking place. The victim is the American journalist, "Míster" Perhaps. It is never made clear whether this scene is real or only a drug-induced vision; its theme of human sacrifice clearly prefigures the story's ending, however. The next day, after arriving at the insurgents' camp, the narrator has to be treated by a physician. He asks for Colonel Reguera, and is calmly told that the Colonel "is busy right now. He still has three more to shoot."[14] In its attempt to conflate ancient Mexican myth with modern events such as the Mexican Revolu-

[13] Darío, *Cuentos fantásticos*, p. 82.
[14] Darío, *Cuentos fantásticos*, p. 87.

tion, Darío's story anticipates a similar approach in contemporary short stories such as the Mexican Carlos Fuentes's "Chac-Mool" (1954) or the Argentine Julio Cortázar's "La noche boca arriba" (1964), of which more will be said in Chapter 7 of this book.

However, it is in "La larva" where Darío unveils some of his deepest fears. The narration unfolds in a spare, unadorned style, as a reminiscence of Darío's youth in Nicaragua. The narrator and protagonist, named Isaac Codomano (who is clearly Darío himself), tells of the ghost stories and superstitions he heard as a child in his native land, and of his own encounter with an apparition. In the darkened streets of his hometown, the fifteen-year-old protagonist, coming home from a serenade in a mood for amorous escapades, sees the figure of a woman wrapped in a shawl. He approaches and propositions her. To his horror, the woman shows herself to be a horrible "larva" – a ghost – with the face of a rotting corpse. Although this tale could easily derive from Darío's readings of baroque Spanish theater (such as Pedro Calderón de la Barca's *El mágico prodigioso* [1637]), the detailed evocation of time and place gives it a powerful confessional resonance that may point to Darío's well-known alcoholic deliriums as well as to psychosexual problems.

Better-known for his mystical and amorous poetry, Amado Nervo also wrote novels and short stories, many of the latter collected in a volume titled *Cuentos misteriosos*. Like Darío, Nervo tended to write introspectively about psychological themes, although his approach is less somber and frequently verges on satire, as in "Don Diego de Noche" (the title alludes to the night-flowering plant *Mirabilis jalapa*). This is the story of a man who, like the Italian symbolist poet Gabrielle D'Annunzio (to whom Nervo alludes in his text), was afraid of decrepitude, and decided never to age beyond his thirty-three years; he finally dies of old age, but his "official" age on his tombstone is still thirty-three. Here Nervo mocks what had already become a cliché of *modernismo* and Decadentism: the notion of "dying young" (expressed in poems such as Nájera's "Para entonces" [When the Time Comes, 1896], Silva's "Nocturno" [1908], and Casal's "La agonía de Petronio" [Petronius' Agony, 1892]). This idea did not signify a distaste for life in most *modernistas* (save, perhaps, for Silva), but expressed instead the ambiguity inherent in the *modernistas*' search for artistic perfection: if "perfection" implies that something is "finished," and if youth is regarded as the "perfect age," then to die young implies a double degree of perfection. Another, more sinister implication is that all perfection is fatal, for it is a harbinger of death.

A satirical thrust reminiscent of Jonathan Swift also underlies many of the best known tales from Lugones's *Las fuerzas extrañas*. Like the eighteenth-century Irish satirist, Lugones shows in these stories a grim and mordant vision of humanity. Lugones's satire is particularly directed at Positivism and its belief in humanity's inherent superiority over nature. The two most frequently reprinted stories of the twelve collected in *Las fuerzas extrañas*, "Los caballos de Abdera" (The Horses of Abdera) and "Yzur," are good examples of Lugones's Swiftian temper. The former, despite its mythical Greco-Roman setting, is evocative of the Houyhnhnms episode in *Gulliver's Travels* (1726); the horses of the Thracian city of Abdera are pampered and educated by their owners to such a degree that they become intelligent and ultimately rebel against their masters. Lugones spoils the tale somewhat at the end by the *deus ex machina* introduction of Hercules, who arrives to save the city from the beasts.

In "Yzur," however, there is no attempt at a "happy ending." It is worth dwelling at length on this story, which is widely regarded as one of the best short stories ever penned by a *modernista*. "Yzur" tells the grim tale of a chimpanzee of the same name bought by a linguist (also the story's narrator) whose enthusiasm for language instruction is reminiscent of George Bernard Shaw's later character of Henry Higgins in *Pygmalion* (1912). Obsessed with proving his theory that "apes were men who for one reason or another had stopped speaking" and that it was therefore possible to give them back speech by means of a series of exercises and disciplines, the scientist subjects Yzur to cruel experiments.[15] Nevertheless, the ape refuses to speak and becomes progressively weaker and more sick. One evening, just before dying, the ape speaks his last and only words: "AMO, AGUA, AMO, MI AMO" ("Master, water, Master, my master"; capitals in the original text).[16]

This story has been read as an expression of Lugones's racism, on the basis of the unfortunate phrase in which the narrator describes the ape's face as that of a "sad old mulatto."[17] It has also been read as a critique of nineteenth-century scientific discourse and as an illustration of Lugones's theosophical ideas, which were undoubtedly important in the development of his poetics.[18] Nevertheless, without excluding these and other interpre-

[15] Leopoldo Lugones, *Las fuerzas extrañas* (Buenos Aires: Ediciones Centurión, 1948), p. 105.

[16] Lugones, *Las fuerzas extrañas*, p. 115.

[17] Lugones, *Las fuerzas extrañas*, p. 114.

[18] See Howard M. Fraser, "Apocalyptic Vision and Modernism's Dismantling of Scientific Discourse: Lugones's 'Yzur'," *Hispania*, 79 (1996), pp. 8–19; and Carmen Ruiz Barri-

tations, "Yzur" can also be read as a fable or allegory about the ethical problems of writing and reading.

It should be noted that the story is largely based on a bilingual pun on the words *simio* (Spanish for "ape"), *singe* (French for "ape"), and *signo* (Spanish for "sign"). This play on words is similar to Rubén Darío's better-known wordplay with the terms *cisne* (Spanish: "swan")/*cygne* (French: "swan")/*signo* in his poem "Los cisnes": "¿Qué signo haces, oh Cisne, con tu encorvado cuello/ al paso de los tristes y errantes soñadores?" ("What sign do you make, O Swan, with your curved neck/ In the presence of sad and wandering dreamers?" Jiménez, p. 211). It might be well to recall here the *modernistas*' penchant for creating a bestiary, or what one might call a "symbolic zoology," in which animals generally become emblems of writing, or of a certain kind of writing. Long before the Mexican poet Enrique González Martínez (1871–1952) opposed the less-frivolous figure of the owl to Darío's symbolic swan, Darío himself had proposed another counterfigure to the swan in his poem "La página blanca" (The Blank Page), in which writing is symbolized by means of the less elegant but more exotic image of a caravan of camels. Lugones's stories in *Las fuerzas extrañas* also abound in animal symbols, and in this sense his book is merely one more link in a chain that also includes Spanish American works such as Horacio Quiroga's *Cuentos de la selva* (Jungle Stories, 1918) and *Anaconda* (1921) and culminates, in a more stylized way, in Julio Cortázar's *Bestiario* (Bestiary, 1951) and Octavio Paz's *El mono gramático* (*The Monkey Grammarian*, 1974).[19]

Another indication of the symbolic link between the ape and writing in

onuevo, "*Las fuerzas extrañas* de Leopoldo Lugones," in *El cuento hispanoamericano*, ed. E. Pupo-Walker (Madrid: Castalia, 1995), pp. 184–9.

19 Using animals as metaphors for writing may seem contradictory at first, since animals themselves do not use language. The metaphor underlines, however, language's "strangeness," its instrumental or thing-like qualities, its apparent inhumanity, despite the fact that it serves as a vehicle for human communication. To make mute entities like a swan, a camel, a snake, or an ape, "speak" is largely what all writers try to do with language when they inscribe equally mute signs upon the blank page. This task is furthermore, violent in more than one way: not only because it tries to break down the barriers between what is natural and what is artificial, but because the very act of writing is itself an action that implies cutting, marking, or tearing an undifferentiated medium. Exploring this view of writing as cutting or mutilation, and proposing analogies with the biological sciences, Jacques Derrida posits the existence of the "textual graft": "One ought to explore systematically not only what appears to be a simple etymological coincidence uniting the graft and the graph (both from *graphion*: writing implement, stylus), but also the analogy between the forms of textual grafting and so-called vegetal grafting, or even, and more commonly today, animal grafting. It would not be enough to compose an encyclopedic catalogue of grafts … one must elaborate a systematic treatise on the textual graft." See

this story is the ape's name. The enigmatic name "Yzur" contains the last two letters of the alphabet (Y and Z) and the particle *Ur*, which in German denotes origins (such as, for example, in the philological term *Ursprache*, which refers to the original language, to the origins of language). Thus the name "Yzur" evokes, simultaneously, language's ending and its beginnings. The inverted ordering (the last letters of the alphabet followed by the particle expressing origins) also anticipates the forcible movement of a return to origins, of the "journey back to the source" in this story, in which the narrator intends to give back to the ape the intelligence he had supposedly lost in some primitive catastrophe.

If we accept the symbolic equation "simian = sign," it is clear that this story dramatizes the violence implicit in every attempt to make signs "speak," to elicit meaning from the written word. In his attempt to develop the ape's ability to produce articulate sounds, the scientist-narrator even goes as far as to stretch the ape's lips with pincers – a method that is all too reminiscent of torture.[20] Nevertheless, the apex of violence is reached when, frustrated in his repeated attempts to make the animal speak, the narrator confesses: "I lost my temper: without thinking twice, I beat him. The only result was tears and absolute silence, unbroken even by moans."[21] With a coldness that seems to prefigure that of the physician-torturers in Nazi concentration camps, Lugones's narrator tells us about the moral suffering he inflicts on the ape, a profound emotional distress caused, according to the narrator, by the ape's own intellectual awakening: "It was clear that he [the ape] was ill and suffering from intelligence and pain."[22] Paradoxically, the closer the narrator seems to be to achieving his goal of making the ape "signify," of making him not only intelligent but *intelligible*, the more the ape suffers, and his suffering is linked, quite tellingly, to a sort of cut or break similar to that of the written word, in his very being: "The abnormal effort demanded of his brain had shattered his organic unity, and sooner or later he would become a hopeless case."[23]

Writing as well as reading in "Yzur" implies a double and contradictory movement of personifying the inhuman and of turning persons into things. As J. Hillis Miller has noted, the very act of writing a novel depends on

Jacques Derrida, *Dissemination*, trans. Barbara Johnson (Chicago: University of Chicago Press, 1981), pp. 202–3.

20 Lugones, *Las fuerzas extrañas*, p. 107.

21 Lugones, *Las fuerzas extrañas*, p. 111.

22 Lugones, *Las fuerzas extrañas*, p. 112.

23 Lugones, *Las fuerzas extrañas*, p. 112.

the attribution of person-like qualities to a linguistic creation.[24] And yet, writers are frequently confronted by the fact that in the very process of writing their narratives their behavior towards their characters, towards those Others whose person-like status they have posited, is inconsistent with the moral principles the narrative claims to uphold. The most obvious and dramatic instance is when authors decide or are forced to represent a character's death, or when they feel that they must portray the suffering of their characters.

It is interesting to note the paradox that, like the ape Yzur, all languages, all writing, despite their impersonal and collective origins, force us to regard them as residues of a human personality and intention. In a grotesque version of the myth of Pygmalion, the narrator-protagonist of "Yzur" attempts to turn the ape into a "person" by "giving it back" its powers of speech. At the same time, however, he insists on performing this task through violent and authoritarian mechanisms by which he ends up turning Yzur into a thing, constantly reminding him that he is an ape and even (as the story suggests) that he is a slave: as we know, the narrator obsessively repeats to Yzur the phrases "I am your master" and "You are my ape."[25] "Yzur" 's narrator wants to personify the ape, but at the same time he wants to bend the ape to his will as if the ape were a thing, not a person, and he is scandalized when the ape resists.

It should be stressed that the ape refuses to signify in the manner the narrator demands of him (that is, by speaking), although the ape's gestures are otherwise highly expressive, which emphasizes even further his condition as a "sign," his proximity to writing. This apparent passivity of the ape-as-writing is implicitly contrasted in the story with the power encoded in the "secret" the ape possesses about the origins of language, as well as in the ape's own brute strength.

The victimization to which both the ape and writing are subjected tends to move the story's focus away from Yzur and centers it instead on the narrator-protagonist, who may well be seen as an allegory of the writer. Paradoxically, it is a literate scientist who performs the acts of violence depicted in the story. It is the scientist's gradual descent into violence, along with the ape's passivity and his assumption of human-like traits, that begins to erode the presumed objectivity of the narrator's discourse and distances the reader from it by raising doubts about the narrator's

24 J. Hillis Miller, *Versions of Pygmalion* (Cambridge, MA: Harvard University Press, 1990), pp. 11, 13, 136.

25 Lugones, *Las fuerzas extrañas*, p. 112.

own sanity. To a certain extent, it might be said that, just as the narrator studies the ape, Lugones himself studies the narrator in the manner of a clinical case. In this sense, the narrator-protagonist of "Yzur" would not be an allegory of all writers, but of a certain kind of writer, perhaps a failed writer, one who is incapable of making signs signify.

However, this failed writer is not Lugones himself. To the contrary, Lugones is indeed successful as a writer, since he is able to produce a memorable text that is laden with meaning and which still "speaks" to us today about a wide range of important issues. Lugones's *tour de force* consists in writing a story full of meaning about the difficulty of producing meaning. The isolation in which both the ape and the scientist find themselves is suggestive in this respect, since, as Jacques Derrida reminds us in *Dissemination* (1981), meaning arises not only from a cut or separation but also from a graft or connection.[26] Solitude turns language into silence, and writing without a context becomes an enigma for the reader.

"Yzur"'s ending is certainly ambiguous: we have only the story's discredited and possibly insane first-person narrator as a witness that the ape finally *did* speak. It is also curious that the ape's first and last words should satisfy so neatly the narrator's needs. In any case, even if we decide not to accept the ending's veracity, seeing it instead as the narrator's fantasy or hallucination, this ending still makes sense in terms of a reading of this story as an allegory of the ethics of writing and reading. The ape's tragic words – "Master, water, Master, my Master" – may well be a reminder that language can only be made to speak, that is to signify, if it is "cared for," that is, if it is given life by means of a personifying operation that "educates" words, linking them to each other in order to create systems of signification. It is a commonplace notion that reading is not productive if the reader lacks an adequate linguistic or contextual background. The ape's plea suggests that writing, despite its violent origins and its resistance to signifying, requires to be treated always with respect, that is, according to its own special and particular way of being, so that it can then carry out its simulation of life and consciousness.

The title of Manuel Díaz Rodríguez's first book of short stories, *Confidencias de Psiquis*, is highly suggestive in terms of the *modernist* tendency toward psychological themes, and indeed most of the stories in the volume have to do with mental aberrations of various sorts, as some of the titles clearly indicate: "Celos" (Jealousy), "Fetiquismo" (Fetishism),

[26] Derrida, *Dissemination*, pp. 202–3.

"Tic," etc. Unlike most other *modernistas*, Díaz Rodríguez had professional first-hand knowledge of psychology through his studies of medicine in Paris and Vienna, and sought to incorporate this knowledge in many of his short stories and in novels such as *Sangre patricia* (Patrician Blood, 1902). Although today he is largely forgotten outside his native Venezuela, Díaz Rodríguez was regarded in the early decades of the twentieth century, along with the Uruguayan José Enrique Rodó, as one of the great masters of Spanish American prose. In the Venezuelan literary tradition, he is recognized as having exerted a strong influence on the young Rómulo Gallegos (1884–1969), Venezuela's foremost twentieth-century novelist.

The stories in Díaz Rodríguez second book, *Cuentos de color* (Stories in Color), were less overtly psychological and more allegorical and "artistic" in the style of Darío's *Azul....* In his later narratives, however, Díaz Rodríguez frequently inserted violent and grotesque scenes which break the superficial harmony of his prose. "Égloga de verano," for example, a story set in a creole ambience, tells the tale of Guacharaco, a small-town sheriff who obstinately courts Justa, the virtuous wife of the peasant Sandalio. One night, as he violently tries to break into Sandalio's house in oder to rape Justa, who is alone, Guacharaco is beheaded by Justa. Díaz Rodríguez's description of this act is sensational in the extreme, but despite its gruesome character the whole scene has an artificial, contrived atmosphere that is still a *modernista* trait: "Guacharaco's head, stretched out in the effort to break in when it was chopped off, jumped, and perhaps in a last convulsion held on with its teeth to the cot's sheet. It was found thus, hanging from the sheet, which undoubtedly did not slip to the ground from the strange weight of the head because it was held tightly on the other side between the cot and the supporting beam of the hut."[27]

Lugones's stories in *Las fuerzas extrañas* and Díaz Rodríguez's later tales such as "Egloga de verano" and "Música bárbara" point toward the transition between the *modernista* short story and the more contemporary forms of the genre found in the works of the Uruguayan Horacio Quiroga (1878–1937). Quiroga, who began his career as a *modernista*, is to the genre of the short story what Julio Herrera y Reissig is to *modernista* verse: a writer who innovates by collecting and intensifying materials and techniques introduced by previous writers. In Quiroga's *Cuentos de amor,*

[27] Manuel Díaz Rodríguez, "Égloga de verano," in *Manuel Díaz Rodríguez*, I. *Colección clásicos venezolanos de la Academia Venezolana de la Lengua, 10* (Caracas: Academia Venezolana de la Lengua, 1964), p. 151.

de locura y de muerte (Stories of Love, Madness, and Death, 1917) we find the *modernista* preoccupation with the psyche and personal identity combined with a more "realist" narrative approach and with the rural or wilderness setting preferred by the later telluric narrative of the Colombian José Eustacio Rivera (1888–1928) and Rómulo Gallegos.

In terms of their themes and allusions, the *modernista* short stories also reflect their authors' insistent bookishness: numerous *modernista* short stories take other literary works as their point of departure – witness Darío's "La larva," which begins with an evocation of Benvenuto Cellini's *Vita* (1562) or Lugones's "La lluvia de fuego" (1906), which is a gloss of the biblical tale of Sodom and Gomorrah. In these and other *modernista* short stories, the setting is frequently an artificial (specifically, philological) re-creation of environments previously encoded in literature – such as the Arcadia of Greek and Roman pastoral poetry, the bohemian world of students and artists of French Romanticism – or of the Orient. Darío's well-known "naturalist" short story "El fardo" (The Bale) in *Azul...* is the exception that proves the rule, since, in the context of the book as a whole, it stands out as an essentially literary experiment in the naturalist style, and is as bookish in its own way as "El velo de la Reina Mab" (Queen Mab's Veil).

Partly because of their extreme subjectivism and concern with subjectivity, the *modernista* short story writers tended to avoid the realist aesthetic in favor of broad stylistic experimentation and a lyrical tone. Unlike their approach to poetry, however, the *modernistas* did not attempt to formulate a poetics of the short story; nevertheless, their stories clearly show the coherent and beneficial impact *modernista* writing had on the Hispanic short story tradition. Through the *modernistas*, the language of the Hispanic short story became more polished, precise, and nuanced, its subjects became more varied, and narrative intensity was emphasized. A greater degree of creative self-consciousness also began to emerge. Indeed, the *modernista* experiments in narrative point of view, tone, and use of symbolic elements in the development of the plot, were contributions adopted even by later Spanish American narrators who wrote in the realist vein. Furthermore, echoes of the *modernistas*' interest in "the fantastic" and in bookish and erudite themes for their short stories may be discerned in the narrative of later Spanish American writers, from Jorge Luis Borges and Alejo Carpentier to Carlos Fuentes and Julio Cortázar.

Further Reading

Mora, Gabriela, *El cuento modernista hispanoamericano: Manuel Gutiérrez Nájera, Rubén Darío, Leopoldo Lugones, Manuel Díaz Rodríguez, Clemente Palma* (Lima–Berkeley: Latinoamericana Editores, 1996). Offers close readings and detailed commentary of the main short story books by Nájera, Darío, Lugones, Díaz Rodríguez, and the Peruvian Clemente Palma (1872–1946), whose work, like Horacio Quiroga's, shades off into the Avant-Garde.

Pupo-Walker, Enrique, "El cuento modernista: su evolución y características," in *Historia de la literatura hispanoamericana*, II. *Del neoclasicismo al modernismo*, ed. Luis Iñigo Madrigal (Madrid, Ediciones Cátedra, 1987), pp. 515–22. A classic summary of the history and development of the *modernista* short story.

Ruiz Barrionuevo, Carmen, "*Las fuerzas extrañas* de Leopoldo Lugones," in *El cuento hispanoamericano*, ed. Enrique Pupo-Walker (Madrid: Editorial Castalia, 1995), pp. 171–90. A very fine overview of Lugones's book in the context of Argentine literary history and the *modernistas*' relation to modernity.

4

The *Modernista* Essay

A rich tradition of Spanish American essayistic writing preceded the *modernistas*, harking back to Colonial times in works of Baroque science and historiography such as the Mexican Carlos de Sigüenza y Góngora's (1645–1700) *Libra astronómica y filosófica* (Astronomical and Philosophical Balance, 1670) and *Alboroto y motín de México* (Uprising and Mutiny in Mexico, 1692), as well as Enlightenment-influenced works of scientific travel and observation such as the Spaniard Alonso Carrió de la Vandera's (1715?–1783) *El lazarillo de ciegos caminantes* (A Guide for Inexperienced Travelers, c. 1776). However, if the essay is regarded as a genre in which ideas, rather than narratives or description, take center stage, then the first great flowering of the Spanish American essay truly takes place during Spanish America's struggle for independence and nation-building, roughly the first two-thirds of the nineteenth century. Key figures in this period are political leaders such as the Venezuelan Simón Bolívar (1783–1830), with his *Manifiesto de Cartagena* (Cartagena Manifesto, 1812) and *Carta de Jamaica* (Letter from Jamaica, 1815), and the Argentine Domingo Faustino Sarmiento (1811–88), with his celebrated work *Civilización y barbarie: vida de Juan Facundo Quiroga* (Civilization and Barbarism: Life of Juan Facundo Quiroga, 1845), as well as humanists and scholars such as the Venezuelan Andrés Bello (1781–1865), whose wide-ranging essayistic work was published mainly in journals he founded and edited, such as *Biblioteca Americana* (1823) and *Repertorio Americano* (1826–27), and the Mexican Ignacio Manuel Altamirano (1834–93), whose essays appeared in his journal *El Renacimiento* (1869).

The *modernistas*' contribution to this tradition, as with the short story, is again connected to their work in journalism, arguably the most programatically modern form of textual production. One of the principal differences between the *modernista* essays and those of their immediate Spanish American predecessors lies precisely in their attitude towards modernity. As I pointed out in Chapter 1, unlike the Spanish American writers of the

Independence and nation-building eras (from Bolívar to Sarmiento), who debated about whether and how to modernize their societies, the *modernistas* felt that they were *already* modern, and they were more concerned with how to effectively express this feeling through literature. *Modernista* essays often promote, celebrate, and analyze literary and cultural modernity.

The *crónica* again played a key role. Many so-called chronicles of Martí, Nájera, Darío, and Gómez Carrillo can in fact be considered essays. Indeed, if the boundary between the *modernista* chronicle and the short story often appears blurred, this is even more evident in the essay. Like the *crónica*, the essay is an expository prose text that makes occasional use of narration and frequently utilizes poetic and rhetorical devices to present its message. Often the essay, like the *crónica*, takes current events as its point of departure. Length is not an important distinguishing factor between these two genres, since it could be argued that book-length essays such as Rodó's *Ariel* (of which more will be said shortly) are actually collections of shorter texts united by a common thread of argument, and there are also book-length chronicles: Darío's *El viaje a Nicaragua* immediately springs to mind, along with many of Gómez Carrillo's travel chronicles.

One important distinction between the two genres lies in their *tone*. Generally, the tone of the *crónicas* is frivolous, superficial, or sensationalist; description prevails over analysis, and ideas are subordinated to events and things. Martí's work, which could be cited as an exception, actually proves the rule, since what stands out in most of the Cuban patriot's *crónicas* is his constant struggle to undermine the superficiality and the sensationalism demanded of him as a journalist by his editors – suffice it to recall the reminder by Bartolomé Mitre y Vedia (editor of the Buenos Aires newspaper *La Nación*) to Martí that his *crónicas* are "merchandise … that is seeking favorable placement."[1]

This conflict is particularly evident in Martí's artistic and literary *crónicas* (following the typology proposed in Chapter 2). In these, he had both to entertain and to enlighten his readers, and the subject matter – new or unknown authors and artists, art exhibits, book reviews – naturally led him toward the essay form. While their introductory nature gives them the status of "news," what makes these texts essayistic is not only their literary or cultural subject matter but also the meditative tone in which they are cast and their abundant digressions, in which Martí reflects on

[1] Cited in Gonzalo de Quesada y Miranda, *Martí, periodista* (Havana: Rambla, Bouza y Comp., 1929), p. 105.

more general social, cultural, or even philosophical questions. Among these chronicles are various highly influential texts Martí wrote to introduce and comment, to his Spanish American readers, on the works of English-speaking authors such as Walt Whitman, Ralph Waldo Emerson, Oscar Wilde, Charles Darwin, and others.

These essay-like chronicles are essentially works of literary and cultural criticism, and in them may be seen the influence of a new, more sophisticated notion of language produced by nineteenth-century philologists as a human artefact, as a thing, among others in the world, endowed with its own historical depth and an almost palpable materiality. This vision of language as an object (frequently, a precious object) led logically to a notion of culture as artifice. Unlike the Romantics, the *modernistas* did not view national culture as a process of spontaneous, natural generation from obscure, folkloric roots. Without forsaking altogether the organic metaphors of romantic philology, the *modernistas*, like their French Symbolist and Decadentist counterparts, regarded national culture (including literature and the arts) as highly refined end-products of a laborious and deliberate historical process. Thus, echoing the ideas of the French literary critic Hippolyte Taine in *Histoire de la littérature anglaise* (History of English Literature, 1864), Martí declared in his 1887 essay on Walt Whitman: "Each stage of society brings its own expression to literature; in such a way, that by the diverse phases of their literature the story of nations might be told with greater truth than through their chronicles and annals."[2]

Much of what was stated about the style of Martí's reportorial chronicles can also be said of his essays. The main qualities of Martí's oratory – sententiousness and use of vivid images – predominate in them, sometimes threatening to overshadow his ideas. Nevertheless, these texts convey an impression of intellectual depth combined with a highly effective, if somewhat baroque, use of language. Conversely, if his essays are oratorical, many of Martí's numerous speeches can also be classified as essayistic, despite their abundant rhetorical flourishes. This is the case with his Steck Hall speech of 1880, and his speeches on José María de Heredia (1803–39) in 1889 and on Simón Bolívar in 1893, as well as with his very famous and highly oratorical text (which was never delivered as a speech), "Nuestra América" ("Our America," 1891).[3]

2 José Martí, *Letras fieras* (Havana: Editorial Letras Cubanas, 1981), p. 498.

3 A fine overview of Martí's speeches and of his power of eloquence is found in Cintio Vitier's "Los discursos de Martí" in Cintio Vitier and Fina García Marruz, *Temas martianos* (Río Piedras: Ediciones Huracán, 1981), pp. 67–91. An example of how the influence of "Nuestra Américas'" has grown over the years is a recent anthology of essays edited by

In "Nuestra América," Martí proposed a theory of culture which synthesized the Romantic idea of culture as an emanation of Nature, with the concept of culture as artifice posited by the widely read and much-admired French philologist Ernest Renan.[4] For Martí, Spanish American culture is the product of a clash between the Europeans' willpower and American Nature (within which Martí also includes the American Indians). This clash has produced deformities in Spanish American culture which must be corrected by seeking a harmony and balance with Nature. To seek such a harmony is for Martí a supremely poetic, creative act: "*Governor*, in a new country, means *Creator*."[5] This culturally deterministic theory of Spanish American literature was further developed and disseminated, as will be seen shortly, by José Enrique Rodó.

Another important oratorical–essayistic text by Martí, among many that could be cited, is his 1882 prologue to *Poema del Niágara* (Poem of Niagara, 1880) by the Venezuelan Juan Antonio Pérez Bonalde (1846–92). On this prologue, Martí, ever the perfectionist, later commented with regret that it was like "new wine," too rich with ideas, that had not fully matured. Nevertheless, this is clearly one of the most remarkable of the many extraordinary essays Martí wrote. "El *Poema del Niágara*" is outstanding because in it Martí offers a vivid (if rather rhapsodic) synthesis of the changes wrought in Spanish American literature and culture by the arrival of modernity:

> There are no permanent works, because works produced during times of realignment and restructuring are shifting and unsettled in their very essence: there are no established paths. The new altars, vast and open as forests, have only just been glimpsed. The mind solicits diverse ideas from everywhere, and those ideas are like coral and starlight and like the waves of the sea. There is a constant yearning

Jeffrey Belnap and Raúl Fernández, *José Martí's "Our America": From National to Hemispheric Cultural Studies* (Durham, NC: Duke University Press, 1998).

4 Paraphrasing liberally from Renan's celebrated 1882 lecture "Qu'est-ce qu'une nation?" Martí summarized Renan's views on national culture in one of his "Escenas europeas" (1884): "Human history is not a chapter in Zoology. Man is a rational and moral being. Free will stands above the base influence of the *Volksgeist*. A nation is a soul, a spiritual principle created out of the past, with its life in the present, and any great assemblage of men of sound minds and generous hearts can create the moral consciousness that constitutes a nation." José Martí, *Obras completas*, vol. 14 (Havana: Editorial Nacional de Cuba, 1963), p. 450.

5 José Martí, "Our America," in *Selected Writings*, ed. Roberto González Echevarría, trans. Esther Allen (New York: Penguin Classics, 2002), p. 290.

> for some knowledge that will confirm current beliefs and a fear of learning something that will alter them.[6]

What first strikes the reader of this essay, however, is its tone, akin to that of a manifesto; "El *Poema del Niágara*" is one of Martí's most sustained attempts at outlining a poetics for *modernismo*. It is a poetics concerned not with technicalities of verse and form, however, but with the philosophical basis for a new literature.

In his comments on Pérez Bonalde's poem (which is not a particularly memorable or *modernista* work itself), Martí seeks to come to terms with his Romantic background and with the ideas of turn-of-the-century Decadence. Martí's Romanticism is by no means a residue of the early and rather weak Hispanic Romanticism of Heredia, Gustavo Adolfo Bécquer, or José Zorrilla (although Martí knew and admired some of their works), but rather the product of his belated and marginal confrontation with the more powerful Anglo-Germanic Romanticism of William Wordsworth, Johann Wolfgang von Goethe, and Samuel Taylor Coleridge. Martí, as a Cuban writer from the latter half of the nineteenth century, deliberately studied the earlier Anglo-Germanic Romanticism because he knew that its ideas had only reached America through their dilute French and Spanish adaptations. Martí's interest in Romanticism does not spring from the nostalgia of a latecomer, however, but from his eclectic search for elements with which to lay the foundations of a solid Spanish American literature.

Another reason for Martí's sympathetic appreciation of Romanticism is his own political agenda: Cuba's independence was to be the culmination of Spanish America's Wars of Independence earlier in the century, which had been highly romantic enterprises themselves at both the practical and ideological levels. On the other hand, Martí wished to maintain a critical distance, both for political and for literary reasons, from French Decadence, which was the literary modality then in vogue: as a political leader, he could hardly believe in "decadence" while preparing a revolution, and as a writer, Martí (like Nietzsche, whose works he probably did not read) viewed Decadence as excessively "effeminate" (he referred to the "decadent" writers as *hembras débiles*, "weak females")[7] and life-denying, and considered it unsuitable to form the basis for the new American literature he wanted to create.

"El *Poema del Niágara*" appears, therefore, as a rather bizarre mixture

6 José Martí, "Prologue to Juan Antonio Pérez Bonalde's *Poem of Niagara*," in *Selected Writings*, pp. 44–6.

7 José Martí, "Prologue to Juan Antonio Pérez Bonalde's *Poem of Niagara*," p. 44.

of Romantic topics and diatribes against Decadence, written in Martí's highly oratorical and image-laden style (which did not escape contamination from Decadentism), leavened with Martí's own perceptive observations (gleaned from his experience of life in New York) about modernity's impact on the life of the mind. Martí's emphasis is on speed, change and uncertainty: "No one nowadays is certain of his faith," he states.[8] Elsewhere in the essay, he observes: "We arise in the morning with one problem, and by the time we go to bed at night we have exchanged it for another. Images devour each other in the mind. There is not enough time to give form to thought."[9] In a visionary passage that Cintio Vitier (b. 1921) has compared with texts by the Peruvian poet César Vallejo (1892–1938), Martí declares of the new poets:

> All have been kissed by the same sorceress. In every one the new blood boils. Men can tear their innermost selves to shreds, but intranquillity, insecurity, vague hopes, and secret visions remain, famished and wrathful, in the most secret recesses of their beings. An immense, pale man, dressed in black, with gaunt face, weeping eyes, and dry lips, is walking gravely across the earth without rest or sleep – and he has taken a seat in every home and has put his trembling hand on every bedstead. Such a pounding in the brain! Such fear in the breast! Such demanding of things that do not come! Such unawareness of what one wants! And in the spirit, such a sense of mingled nausea and delight: nausea for the day that is dying, delight for the dawn![10]

Martí sees the birth of the new writers and intellectuals as an agonizing process; writers must discard old habits (such as, the slow, methodical accumulation of knowledge in an atmosphere of peaceful meditation) and must become accustomed instead to working in a more mundane ambience, suffering the continuous and often rending friction of everyday life, and facing an ever-increasing mass of unrefined information. "El *Poema del Niágara*," is above all a diagnosis of the crisis of turn-of-the-century writers in Europe as well as Spanish America. Despite its manifesto-like style, it makes few concrete proposals about how the future Spanish American literature must be, save that it should not fall into the trap of Decadence and should not abandon the metaphysical, transcendentalist search for unity and harmony in the cosmos that was, in Martí's view, the Romantics' greatest legacy.

8 José Martí, "Prologue to Juan Antonio Pérez Bonalde's *Poem of Niagara*," p. 44.
9 José Martí, "Prologue to Juan Antonio Pérez Bonalde's *Poem of Niagara*," p. 46.
10 José Martí, "Prologue to Juan Antonio Pérez Bonalde's *Poem of Niagara*," p. 44.

Martí's unexpected death on the battlefields of Cuba in 1895 left his literary legacy almost as scattered as his political legacy. Given the turbulence of the times, there would be no attempt to collect Martí's enormous output of *crónicas*, essays, letters, and poetry until his disciple Gonzalo de Quesada y Aróstegui's first attempt in *Martí, Obras reunidas*, published in 15 volumes between 1900 and 1919. "Nuestra America," now considered a key work in Martí's essayistic *oeuvre*, along with "El *Poema del Niágara*," were mostly inaccessible to Cuban and Spanish American readers of the early 1900s. The way was thus open for other, younger *modernistas* to make their mark in the essay genre.

Although many *crónicas* can be considered essays, certain *modernista* prose writers and poets also wrote essays *tout court*, although they are less remembered for this: such is the case of the Uruguayan novelist Carlos Reyles (1868–1938) with his Nietzschean essays in *La muerte del cisne* (The Death of the Swan, 1910) or of Lugones's explorations of Argentine history in *El imperio jesuítico* (The Jesuit Empire, 1904). Nevertheless, *modernismo* also produced several writers devoted almost exclusively to the essay as a genre, who attempted to distinguish their essays clearly from the ubiquitous *crónicas*. Foremost among these is José Enrique Rodó, followed by other less remembered authors, such as the Peruvians Manuel González Prada and Ventura García Calderón (1887–1960), the Venezuelan Rufino Blanco-Fombona (1874–1944), and the Colombians Carlos Arturo Torres (1867–1911) and Baldomero Sanín Cano (1861–1957).

Though it is true that all the major *modernistas* were acquainted to a greater or lesser degree with philology as a discipline, in the form either of literary criticism or of grammatical and lexicographical studies, the only major *modernista* who can be considered a professional philologist is Rodó. Despite his many incursions into Uruguayan politics, Rodó's most constant occupation was what today would be termed "cultural criticism" (criticism of values and ideologies), and literary criticism. Rodó's allegiance to philology as a discipline, combined with his political and moral preoccupations, led him to prefer the essay over narrative fiction or journalism. Although he wrote the chronicles collected posthumously in *El camino de Paros*, a large portion of his work consists of critical essays written in a solemn style and measured tone meant to highlight the profundity of his ideas.

The works of Renan and Taine – one a standard-bearer for Romantic philology, the other for positivist literary history – were both incorporated, and to a certain extent reconciled, in the work of Rodó. Despite being the co-founder in 1895 of a journal with the positivist-sounding title of

Revista Nacional de Literatura y Ciencias Sociales (National Review of Literature and Social Sciences), Rodó was sympathetic to the *modernistas*' aestheticism. Indeed, his first important essay, "El que vendrá" (He who Is to Come, 1896), is a lyrical and – paradoxically – rather detached meditation on the different attitudes taken by writers at the turn of the nineteenth century toward the feeling of "decadence" that was widespread in Western culture. Renan and Taine are mentioned together in that essay because of their common interest in – to use Rodó's terms – the "Cult of Truth." The essay, which ends with a call for a new artistic leadership, for a sort of literary Messiah, is preceded by an epigraph from Renan in a style evocative of the French philologist's famous "Prière sur l'Acropole" (1876).

On the other hand, throughout Rodó's critical work, the Tainean emphasis on environmental determinism reappears, as well as his concept of "representative" artists. Two of Rodó's best critical essays, "Juan María Gutiérrez y su época" (Juan María Gutiérrez and His Times) and "Montalvo" (both from 1913), follow Taine's method of historico-literary reconstruction. Significantly, in his well-known essay on "Rubén Darío. Su personalidad literaria. Su última obra" (Rubén Darío, his Literary Personality and His Latest Work, 1899), Rodó criticizes the Nicaraguan poet's fascination with Decadentism in *Prosas profanas* with the assertion: "No es el poeta de América" ("He is not America's poet"); in other words, denying Darío's status as an artist representative of his time and place. It should be pointed out that Rodó had many other critics as his models; among them, the Uruguayan Juan María Gutiérrez (1807–78), the Spaniards Marcelino Menéndez Pelayo, Juan Valera, the Countess Pardo Bazán, and *Clarín*, and the Frenchmen Sainte-Beuve, Marie-Jean Guyau, Ferdinand Brunetière, Anatole France, and Paul de Saint-Victor.

Rodó's two most outstanding books of essays, by far, are *Motivos de Proteo* – which synthesizes Rodó's "ethics of becoming," according to Pedro Henríquez Ureña (1884–1946) – and the well-known and highly influential *Ariel*. Like Martí's essays, *Ariel* owes much of its rhetoric and structure to the oratorical tradition. The book is in fact presented, in the framing tale that serves as prologue and epilogue, as a long valedictory speech given by an "old and revered teacher," nicknamed "Próspero" by his students because he habitually gave his lectures sitting next to a statue of the character Ariel from Shakespeare's *The Tempest* (1611). Originally published as an integral work, *Ariel* may be divided into six sections, besides the prologue and the epilogue. These divisions were suggested by Rodó himself after the publication of *Ariel*, when he wrote a summary of the book's content at the request of a friend. Sections 1 to 4 deal with such classic turn-of-the-nineteenth-century topics as the cult of youth, or the appeal to youth as a force for cultural and social innovation; the need for an organic cultural development; the conflict between the self and the outside world; the concept of Beauty in culture; the relationship between beauty and morality; the rise of utilitarianism; the relationship between utilitarianism and democracy, and the need for a redefinition of democracy that will avoid confusion with "the rule of mediocrity" (in Rodó's phrase). As an illustration of this issue of utilitarianism and democracy, sections 5 and 6 offer a detailed – if, on occasion, factually inaccurate – critique of the civilization of the United States. The crisis of 1898 brought about by the Spanish American War made these comments on the United States particularly opportune, and they are partially responsible for the book's popularity in Spanish America as well as for the controversial reputation it has retained to this day.

In *Ariel*, Rodó tried to outline a program of action for the Spanish American intellectuals of his generation. *Ariel*'s enormous impact on its Spanish American readership was due not only to the ideas it expressed, but also to its programmatic, manifesto-like quality, and to its oratorical rhetoric. There are various styles of oratory, as is well known, and that of Próspero in *Ariel* is one of measured and rational exhortation, unlike Martí's more fiery and poetic style. So balanced and polished is Rodó's style in *Ariel*, that it is easy to forget that its author was only twenty-nine years old when the book was published. Donning the mask of Próspero, Rodó manages to sound like a wise old sage communicating an ancient and unquestionable wisdom.

It should also be noted that Rodó made certain that his work was read and commented on by nearly all the major Hispanic intellectuals of his day, from Juan Valera and Miguel de Unamuno in Spain, to the young Pedro Henríquez Ureña and Alfonso Reyes (1889–1959) in Mexico. Rodó sent copies of his book to all of them and wrote asking for their opinion of his work. Through the years, *Ariel* has inspired a long lineage of essays that echo its arguments or reply to them, from *La creación de un continente* (The Creation of a Continent, 1912) by Francisco García Calderón (1880–1953), through Alfonso Reyes's *Última Tule* (1941), to *Calibán. Apuntes sobre la cultura en nuestra América* (Caliban: Notes on Culture in Our America, 1972) by Roberto Fernández Retamar (b. 1930).

If Ariel in Rodó's text is a figure of the purity and perfection to which the *modernista* artists and intellectuals aspired, in his second major work, *Motivos de Proteo*, Rodó's tutelary deity is very different and in some ways more problematic. Proteus, the variously shaped keeper of Neptune's flocks in Greco-Roman myth, was an ambiguous symbol of magic and power but also of instability and change. Ever since the Renaissance, the figure of Proteus in his better aspect, that of the "civic Proteus," came to symbolize the seemingly unlimited powers of humanistic knowledge. In the writings of Pico della Mirandola (in his *Oratio de hominis dignitate*) and of Juan Luis Vives, among others, the ideal of the *uomo universale* is associated with the myth of Proteus, since one of the principal aims of the Neoplatonic humanists of the Renaissance, such as Pico and Ficino, was to show how the forms of multiplicity were resolved into unity.[11] Centuries later, nineteenth-century philologists – the spiritual heirs of Renaissance humanism – evoked once again the figure of Proteus, and this would become disseminated throughout the culture as a whole, leaving its mark on journalism (as may be seen in Nájera's many pseudonyms) as well as on the novel. It should not be surprising, then, that the most "philological" of the *modernistas* should choose as his emblem the figure of the mythical shepherd of Neptune's flocks. Proteus symbolizes for Rodó philology itself, because of philology's wondrous capacity to imitate its object of inquiry and resurrect bygone eras; in Rodó's words:

> That inherent multiplicity which is part of human nature, is in our time more intense than ever. ... From the time that has died, from long-gone humanity, we not only receive many and diverse influences due to the complexity of our ethnic origins, but those influences are multiplied thanks to that wonderful sense of historical empathy, to that second life of the past that has been, one of the most interesting developments of the last one hundred years, and has shed an almost-prophetic light on intellectual activity. No other age has understood, like ours, the souls of past civilizations and has raised them to a new life by means of the wizardry of imagination and feeling. By these means, the past is for us an influence that can impose upon us deep and tenacious suggestions, not limited, as with the Renaissance, to the legacy and genius of a single civilization, but coming from wherever humanity has pursued its ideals and poured its spirit into new and more energetic molds.[12]

[11] A. Bartlett Giamatti, "Proteus Unbound: Some Versions of the Sea God in the Renaissance," in *The Disciplines of Criticism: Essays in Literary Theory, Interpretation, and History*, ed. Peter Demetz, Thomas Greene, and Lowry Nelson (New Haven and London: Yale University Press, 1967), pp. 438–40.

[12] Cited by Emir Rodríguez Monegal in "Introducción general," in José Enrique Rodó, *Obras completas* (Madrid: Aguilar, 1967), p. 109.

It should also be remembered that Ariel, in Rodó's text, appears not as Shakespeare's "airy sprite," but as the statue which adorns Próspero's study; by adopting Proteus as a symbol, Rodó is clearly seeking a less stiff and one-dimensional emblem for his "ethics of becoming." However, the "numen del mar" ("spirit of the sea," as Rodó calls him) is also a sign that stands for the instability and mutability of human nature through time. This deep sense of time's flow is one of the most striking differences between *Motivos de Proteo* and Rodó's earlier essays, which tended toward an ontology based on stony permanence. "Time is the supreme innovator," Rodó declares, and later he states:

> We persist only in the continuity of our modifications; in the more or less regular order that controls them; in the force that thrusts us forward towards the most mysterious and transcendent transformation of all. ... We are the ship's wake, whose material essence does not remain the same for two successive instants because it dies and is reborn unceasingly from the waves; the wake that is not a persistent reality but a moving shape, a sequence of rythmic impulses that act upon a constantly renewed object.[13]

The problem with which Rodó grapples in *Motivos de Proteo* is how the self can survive in a changing world, in the midst of circumstances which constantly threaten its integrity. If change is inevitable, and "conversion" is the normal state of human existence, how can the self control change, and control itself? From a more literary standpoint, how can a writing based on the primacy of the self survive in an age of constant flux and transition? It is the recognition of this dilemma (not the solutions he offers, however) that makes Rodó a truly modern writer.

Leaving aside his extremely important role as a "cultural critic" in works such as *Ariel* and *Motivos de Proteo*, Rodó's originality in the history of Spanish American essayism and literary criticism lies in his belief that criticism is a form of artistic creation, and that as such, it is worthy of special respect. For Rodó, criticism was not merely a belletristic pastime or a covert way to discuss politics, but (in his words) "the most vast and complex of literary genres."[14] The ideal critic, according to Rodó in his posthumous *Ultimos motivos de Proteo* (1932), is a *homo duplex* who is capable of intuitively identifying with the work of art and of re-creating it by means of commentary and paraphrase, while simultaneously judging the value of the work dispassionately.

13 José Enrique Rodó, *Obras completas* (Madrid: Aguilar, 1967), pp. 309–11.
14 Rodó, *Obras completas*, p. 169.

Rodó's insistence on criticism's artistic side should not be understood simply as an attempt to purposely blur the distinction between criticism and fiction, but as a statement of criticism's inherent value. Terms such as "art" and "artistic" had connotations at the turn of the nineteenth century which were somewhat different from those of today, and when Rodó speaks of an "artistic" criticism he is referring not only to an unfathomable "creative" element, but also to the intellectual precision and stylistic polish he felt criticism should have – to what today we would call "professionalism." Rodó did more than any other *modernista* to exalt literary criticism to its full dignity as an autonomous discipline. It was his respect for the "purity" of criticism that led him to avoid placing it, as his Romantic predecessors had done, fully in the service of a "national consciousness." When Rodó, like many other *modernistas* after 1898, felt the need to define once more the nature of Spanish American culture, he did so in works of "cultural criticism" such as *Ariel*, *Motivos de Proteo*, and *Liberalismo y jacobinismo* (1906), rather than in works of strictly literary criticism and scholarship.

The rather strict distinction Rodó wished to maintain between cultural criticism and literary criticism tends to break down, of course, when his work and that of other *modernista* essayists is more closely scrutinized. The gnawing question that underlies most Spanish American essay-writing since Bello is that of Spanish American culture's uniqueness and originality. At least since Martí and Rodó, this uniqueness is traced to the peculiarity of Spanish American culture vis-à-vis that of Europe. In Rodó's essays, for example, as in those of the other *modernistas*, one can see, two phases: a "cosmopolitan," and an "Americanist" one. Until the crisis of 1898, Rodó, like Darío, seemed to regard Spanish America mainly as a backward province of European culture; the problem for Spanish American literature seemed to be how to "catch up" with the literature of the "civilized nations." After 1898, however, Rodó and other *modernistas* moved to a position similar to that of Martí in "Nuestra América": Spanish American literature's uniqueness lay in the harmonious and creative interaction between a Europeanized consciousness and the Nature and indigenous peoples of America. (The fact that such harmony was virtually nonexistent did not prevent the *modernistas* from making it their ultimate goal.) This is essentially what Rodó preached in *Ariel*, although being from the more Europeanized River Plate region, he paid virtually no heed to the Indians, emphasizing instead the vision of a "regenerated America" (in his words) based on a fusion – achieved by a young and educated elite – of Hispanic and French culture in the ideal of "Latinity."

A Peruvian precursor of *modernismo*, Manuel González Prada enunciated in 1886, fourteen years before Rodó's appeal to youth in *Ariel*, a similar creed which he summarized with the slogan: "Los viejos a la tumba; los jóvenes a la obra" ("The old ones to the grave; the young ones to their work"). González Prada was, however, a very different sort of essayist from Rodó. A caustic freethinker with anarchist leanings, González Prada was a polemicist who collected many of his intensely critical essays and (inevitably) speeches in books with such characteristic titles as *Páginas libres* (Free Pages, 1894), *Horas de lucha* (Hours of Battle, 1908), and the posthumous *El tonel de Diógenes* (Diogenes's Barrel, 1945). González Prada is also remembered as one of the first Peruvian intellectuals to call attention to the plight of the Indians, in *Nuestros indios* (Our Indians, 1904). However, one of his most interesting essays from a literary-historical perspective is "Junto a Renan" (1894), in which González Prada narrates his personal acqaintance with the French philologist (he attended Renan's courses in Oriental Philology at the Collège de France) and attests to the strong influence of philology on *modernista* writing.

It is worth dwelling briefly on González Prada's account of his meeting with Renan, because it is in many ways emblematic of the complexities involved in the *modernistas*' approach to the European writers who were their models. As González Prada narrates:

> I went on a Wednesday to the *Hall of Oriental Languages*, and no sooner had I sat down, than Renan entered the room. I made as if to leave; but he, without opening his lips, gestured with his right hand that I could stay. Interpreting his gesture as: *Stay, but be quiet*, I nodded silently to express my thanks. We both sat down, he at the head of the table and with his back to the fireplace, I at his left side, in the same seat I had taken before his arrival. He unpacked his roll of papers, I opened my book; he began to read, and I did the same.
>
> On many other occasions we found ourselves alone with each other, quite close, almost brushing each other's knees, and we never said a word to each other. Sometimes he would interrupt his reading, leaving his papers aside, and laid his eyes on me. Certain that he was gazing at me without seeing me, I fixed my eyes on him and examined him from head to toe.[15]

This mirror-like and silent confrontation between the elegant Peruvian gentleman and the rumpled and obese French writer summarizes the drama

[15] Manuel González Prada, "Junto a Renan," in *Nuevas páginas libres* (Santiago de Chile: Ediciones Ercilla, 1937), pp. 121–2.

of *modernismo*'s relationship to European literature: suspicious admiration on the Spanish American's part, and the supreme indifference of the European before the other's searching gaze. Significantly, this is a scene of reading; both men are reading, and it could be said that they are reading *each other*. At least, González Prada reads Renan, since he is certain that Renan is not reading him. More interestingly, perhaps, nothing apparently happens. Renan and González Prada occupy the same room but not the same ontological plane, so to speak. They do not touch, there is no contact between them. (Earlier in his text, González Prada says that, paradoxically, he and Renan had been "like two friends who were never aware of their friendship.")[16] But this is, of course, a mystification in González Prada's account. In a typically *modernista* (and modern) gesture, González Prada isolates one moment, one potentially significant instant, and invites us to consider it. Although he informs his readers that he attended Renan's courses in Oriental philology in the Collège de France in 1891 and 1892, González Prada never speaks about the history of his relation to Renan, how he came to know of his work, and how and why Renan's work is important to him. González Prada does not do this, probably because it would imply discussing the process that led to his writing the essay "Junto a Renan," and doing so would imply recognizing his debt to Renan. This would, in turn, place him at a disadvantage, display his weakness, and weaken the effect of that scene of reading in which, reversing roles, González Prada was able to examine Renan like Renan would have examined him (if he had been interested): as a museum specimen. Ultimately, González Prada's essay unveils the tensions in which *modernista* writing was constituted, tensions that encompassed not only the relation between America and Europe, but also that between the fictions of literature and the truth-claims of philology.

Other *modernista* essayists in the early years of the twentieth century followed Rodó's lead. Rufino Blanco-Fombona's work, for instance, evinces the almost missionary zeal and broad "Americanist" perspective implicit in Rodó's "Arielism," as some of his titles attest: *Letras y letrados de Hispanoamérica* (Literature and Men of Letters of Spanish America, 1908), *Grandes escritores de América* (Great Writers of America, 1917), and *El modernismo y los poetas modernistas* (*Modernismo* and the *modernista* poets, 1929). The name of the highly successful publishing house that Blanco-Fombona founded in Madrid in 1914 is equally telling: Editorial América. Two of its main series of publications were the "Biblioteca

16 González Prada, "Junto a Renan," p. 121.

Andrés Bello," which published Spanish American literary works, and the "Biblioteca Ayacucho," devoted mostly to nineteenth-century Spanish American history.

Closer to Rodó in age and inclinations was Carlos Arturo Torres, whose book *Idola fori. Ensayo sobre las supersticiones políticas* (Idola Fori: An Essay on Political Superstitions, 1910) appeared with a laudatory prologue from Rodó himself. Torres was an anglophile who had earlier published a series of essays on English literature entitled *Estudios ingleses* (1907). Following Sir Francis Bacon's incipient theory of ideologies in his *Novum Organum* (1620), Torres wrote what is essentially the first serious study of ideology in Spanish American culture and politics. Curiously, for a critic of ideology Torres was rather dogmatic himself, and this is reflected in the highly assertive but colorless style of his book.

Another Colombian essayist, Baldomero Sanín Cano, though ten years his senior, was a kindred spirit to Rodó. Like the Uruguayan, Sanín Cano was primarily a literary and cultural critic. He had read more widely than Rodó himself, and possessed a broad knowledge of German and Italian literature. His acquaintance with English literature was particularly intimate, since, like Andrés Bello, Sanín Cano had lived for a long period in Great Britain (he taught Spanish language and literature at Edinburgh University). Perfectly bilingual in Spanish and English, he collaborated in the *Modern English Review*. On his return to Colombia, he found time after his duties as Minister of Finance to write the brief and elegant essays of cultural and literary criticism collected in *La civilización manual y otros ensayos* (The Handy Civilization and Other Essays, 1925), *Indagaciones e imágenes* (Investigations and Images, 1927), and *Crítica y arte* (Criticism and Art, 1932).

No less tenacious in his desire to promote a renewed "Americanism" without losing touch with the European cultural legacy was Ventura García Calderón. Unlike Torres's and Sanín Cano's anglophilia, García Calderón's work exemplified the "Pan-Latin" link with France for which Rodó repeatedly called. A long-time resident of Paris, he began writing *crónicas* in the style of Enrique Gómez Carrillo. Many of his narrative works were written directly in French. Among his salient essayistic works dealing with Spanish American literature are: *Del romanticismo al modernismo. Poetas y prosistas* peruanos (From Romanticism to *Modernismo*: Peruvian Poets and Prose Writers, 1910) and *La literatura peruana* (Peruvian Literature, 1914). García Calderón's essays, like Blanco-Fombona's or Sanín Cano's, frequently consisted of "profiles" and review essays of contemporary Spanish American writers, which were meant to promote the synthesis of

"Americanism" and European aestheticism that lay at the core of Rodó's call to renew Spanish American culture.

As has been seen, the *modernista* essay was, from the beginning, closely allied to the *crónica*, but by the early years of the twentieth century it acquired an identity of its own in the works of José Enrique Rodó and his many followers. These essays are distinguished from those of earlier periods in Spanish American literary history by their deep concern with the phenomenon of modernity, with its promises and its perils. From Martí to Rodó, the *modernistas* not only celebrated modernity in their essays but also reflected gravely on the changes wrought by modernity on two areas of special concern to them: literature and politics. Furthermore, two important veins of early twentieth-century Spanish American essay-writing are derived from the *modernistas*' essays: modern literary criticism and scholarship, as exemplified by the works of the Mexican Alfonso Reyes and the Dominican Pedro Henríquez Ureña, and essays of social and cultural interpretation by authors such as the Peruvian José Carlos Mariátegui (1895–1930), the Argentine Ezequiel Martínez Estrada (1895–1964), and the Puerto Rican Antonio S. Pedreira (1899–1939).

Further Reading

Belnap, Jeffrey and Raúl Fernández, *José Martí's "Our America": From National to Hemispheric Cultural Studies* (Durham, NC: Duke University Press, 1998). An anthology of essays by various critics that take "Nuestra America" as their point of departure for a variety of views on Martí and his relation to the United States. Particularly noteworthy is the essay "José Martí and the Heroic Image" by Oscar R. Martí (no relation), which proposes that Martí's heroic stature in Spanish American politics and culture is fundamentally due to his literary genius.

González Echevarría, Roberto, "The Case of the Speaking Statue: *Ariel* and the Magisterial Rhetoric of the Latin American Essay," in *The Voice of the Masters: Writing and Authority in Modern Latin American Literature* (Austin: University of Texas Press, 1985), pp. 8–32. A highly suggestive deconstructive reading of *Ariel* which posits that its long-lasting influence is due less to Rodó's anti-US polemic than to its implicit authoritarian rhetoric.

San Román, Gustavo, *This America we Dream Of: Rodó and* Ariel *One Hundred Years On* (London: Institute of Latin American Studies, 2001). An essay commemorating the centennial of *Ariel* and tracing its influence on modern Latin American thought.

5

The *Modernista* Novel

In view of the key role played by prose writings in the development of *modernismo*, it is not surprising that the *modernistas* also contributed greatly to the genre of the novel in Spanish America. The *modernista* legacy to the Spanish American novel is significant and extensive, despite the fact that the *modernistas* did not predominate in this genre as they did in poetry, or in their *crónicas* and short stories. As Max Henríquez Ureña points out, in Spanish America "after the 1880s, novelistic production increases in quantity and importance."[1] Supported by a tradition dating back to the Independence period (in works such as José Joaquín Fernández de Lizardi's *El Periquillo Sarniento* [The Mangy Parrot, 1816]) the novelistic genre flourished owing to many of the same socioeconomic conditions that contributed to the rise of *modernismo* – political stability, the growth of the cities, the rise of mass journalism. The *modernista* novels were, quite simply, important components of a broad novelistic "boom" that occurred in Spanish America around the turn of the nineteenth century, which also encompassed novels written in other modalities, such as *criollismo* (Creolism) or the French-derived modes of Naturalism and Decadence. A cursory survey of literary histories by Fernando Alegría (1918–2005), Enrique Anderson Imbert (1910–2000), Cedomil Goic (b. 1928), Arturo Uslar Pietri (1906–2001), Luis Alberto Sánchez (1900–94), and Max Henríquez Ureña (1885–1968) produces a list of some forty *modernista* novels, from Martí's *Lucía Jerez* (originally titled *Amistad funesta* [Fatal Friendship], 1885) to Carlos Reyles's *El embrujo de Sevilla* (*Castanets*, 1927).[2] Recent scholarship has also uncovered the earliest *modernista*

[1] Max Henríquez Ureña, *El retorno de los galeones* (Madrid: Renacimiento, 1930), p. 58.

[2] See Fernando Alegría, *Historia de la novela hispanoamericana* (Mexico: Ediciones de Andrea, 1965); Enrique Anderson Imbert, *Historia de la literatura hispanoamericana*, 2 vols (Mexico: Fondo de Cultura Económica, 1965); Cedomil Goic, *Historia de la novela hispanoamericana* (Valparaiso, Chile: Ediciones Universitarias, 1972); Arturo Uslar Pietri,

novel, *Por donde se sube al cielo* (Where One Rises to Heaven, 1882), written by Manuel Gutiérrez Nájera.[3]

The *modernista* novels arose and developed during a period of approximately forty years, between the last two decades of the nineteenth century and the first two decades of the twentieth. However, these novels are not evenly distributed throughout those four decades: only nine important *modernista* novels were published during the first seventeen years of the period, from 1882 to 1899, while in the following fourteen years, from 1900 to 1915, there are twenty. (These novels' geographic distribution is more uniform – at least in terms of their authors' country of origin: they are produced in the Southern Cone as well as in the Antilles and Central America.) The apparent increase in the production of *modernista* novels at the beginning of the twentieth century may simply have been due to the fact that *modernismo* was reaching the apogee of its diffusion, but it may also be related to extraliterary events such as the Spanish–Cuban–

Breve historia de la novela hispanoamericana (Caracas: Ediciones Edime, 1954); Luis Alberto Sánchez, *Proceso y contenido de la novela hispanoamericana* (Madrid: Gredos, 1968); Max Henríquez Ureña, *Breve historia del modernismo* (Mexico: Fondo de Cultura Económica, 1954). In chronological order by year of publication or date of writing, this list (which is not exhaustive) includes the following works: José Martí, *Lucía Jerez* (originally titled *Amistad funesta* [Fatal Friendship], 1885); Amado Nervo, *El bachiller* (The Student, 1896); José Asunción Silva, *De sobremesa* (After-Dinner Talk, 1896); Rubén Darío, *El hombre de oro* (The Man of Gold, 1897); Pedro César Dominicci, *La tristeza voluptuosa* (Voluptuous Sadness, 1899), *El triunfo del ideal* (Triumph of the Ideal, 1901), and *Dyonisios* (1904); Enrique Gómez Carrillo, *Maravillas* (Marvels, 1899), *Del amor, del dolor y del vicio* (Of Love, Pain, and Vice, 1899), and *El evangelio del amor* (The Gospel of Love, 1922); José María Vargas Vila, *Ibis* (1899) and *Rosas de la tarde* (Afternoon Roses, 1900); Emilio Rodríguez Mendoza, *Ultima esperanza* (Last Hope, 1899), *Vida nueva* (New Life, 1902), *Días romanos* (Roman Days, 1906), and *Cuesta arriba* (1908); Carlos Reyles, *La raza de Caín* (The Race of Cain, 1900); Manuel Díaz Rodríguez, *Ídolos rotos* (Broken Idols, 1901) and *Sangre patricia* (Patrician Blood, 1902); José María Rivas Groot, *Resurrección* (Resurrection, 1901); Juan Guerra Núñez, *Vae solis* (1905); Ángel de Estrada, *Redención* (Redemption, 1906) and *El triunfo de las rosas* (The Triumph of the Roses, 1918); Rufino Blanco-Fombona, *El hombre de hierro* (1907); Alfonso Hernández-Catá, *Novela erótica* (Erotic Novel, 1907) and *El ángel de Sodoma* (The Angel of Sodom, 1920); Enrique Larreta, *La gloria de don Ramiro* (The Glory of Don Ramiro, 1908); Emilio Cuervo Márquez, *Phinées* (1909); Abraham Valdelomar, *La ciudad de las tísicas* (The City of Consumptive Women, 1911), *Neuronas* (Neurons, 1918), and *La ciudad muerta* (The Dead City, 1911); Eduardo Barrios, *El niño que enloqueció de amor* (The Boy who Became Crazed with Love, 1913); Tulio Manuel Cestero, *La sangre* (Blood, 1913); Pedro Prado, *La reina de Rapa Nui* (The Queen of Rapa Nui, 1914) and *Alsino* (1920); Luis Felipe Rodríguez, *Cómo opinaba Damián Paredes* (The Opinions of Damián Paredes, 1916) and *La conjura de la Ciénaga* (The Conspiracy of the *Ciénaga*, 1923).

3 Manuel Gutiérrez Nájera, *Obras*, XI. *Narrativa I: Por donde se sube al cielo (1882)*, ed. Ana Elena Rodríguez Alejo, Prologue by Belem Clark de Lara (Mexico: Universidad Nacional Autónoma de México, 1994).

American War of 1898, which, as we have noted, had a significant effect on the *modernistas*.

What are the main traits that distinguish the *modernista* novels from the *criollista*, Naturalist, and Decadentist novels published during the same period? How important is the *modernistas*' legacy in this genre? In terms of their writing, all the *modernista* novels make use of the so-called "artistic prose" pioneered by Martí and Nájera in their chronicles, stories, and essays, and later codified by Enrique Gómez Carrillo in his 1919 essay "El arte de trabajar la prosa" (The Art of Working With Prose). This concept is derived, in turn, from the *modernistas*' philological view of language as an object, with a history and a concreteness of its own, which allows words to be manipulated as "collectables," purely for their aesthetic value, without being totally subordinated to their signifying function. "Artistic prose" was always harmonious, sensuous, meticulously descriptive, full of eye-catching phrases, and was supposed to possess perennial value. The *modernistas* frequently used terms such as "solid," "polished," "pure," and "marble-like" (*marmóreo*) to refer to this style, which, though brilliant at its best, could often become exceedingly hieratic and lifeless.

The *modernista* novels also display most of the recurrent topics common to *modernista* writings: the interior, the museum, the library, the *femme fatale*, the dandy, and the sense of *spleen*, among others. However, it is at the ideological level that the *modernista* novel most clearly differentiates itself from the *criollista* and Naturalist novels (more will be said about Decadentism below). The ideology of the *modernista* novels is profoundly antipositivistic and critical. As was said earlier, *modernista* writing arises from a critical, philological awareness of the artificiality of language; the *modernista* novel extends that critical approach to the ideological framework that sustains both the *criollista* and Naturalist novels. Even as they incorporate characters, themes, and topics derived from Naturalism, the *modernista* novels question Naturalism's attempt to explain, by means of scientific models, a reality that seems to be ever more fluid and chaotic. This does not imply that *modernista* novelists rejected the sociopolitical thrust of naturalist fiction; indeed, that was an aspect of Naturalism in which they were deeply interested. However, the *modernistas* approached the issue of the relationship between the literary work and its social context with cautious skepticism. The cosmopolitan and urban ambience of most *modernista* novels is also in part due to this skeptical attitude, which led them to distrust the facile idealization of the countryside typical of most *criollista* fiction.

At first, it might seem that *modernista* novels are essentially a Spanish

American version of the European "Decadent" novels in the mold of J. K. Huysman's *À rebours*. However, although "Decadence" – sociopolitical, cultural, or moral – and "art for art's sake" were recurrent topics in the *modernista* novels, the *modernistas'* Decadentism was always highly ironic and self-conscious. Decadentism, it should be remembered, was largely stimulated by nineteenth-century physics's idea of entropy and its extension to history and society as a sort of "social thermodynamics": it was believed that just as all systems tend to move in the direction of increasing disorder, each society's "progress" must reach a peak and then give way to an inevitable decline. However, even the most ardent Decadentists among the Spanish American *modernistas*, such as José Asunción Silva and Julián del Casal, understood that their attitude had little correspondence with their Spanish American sociohistorical milieu. They were well aware that from a European point of view, America – both North and South – was still the paradigm of a raw new society full of untapped energy. This awareness is reflected in the *modernista* novels, and thus makes their "Decadentism" rather suspect. For example, José Fernández, the protagonist of Silva's *De sobremesa*, although fascinated by the turn-of-the-century Decadent art and lifestyle, nevertheless possessed, we are told, "an athlete's physique," unlike his model, the weakling Des Esseintes from *À rebours*.[4] Fernández was in fact a hyperactive *rastaquouère*, one of those wealthy South Americans who tried to buy their way into the higher levels of French society at the turn of the nineteenth century.

A consideration of the protagonist in the *modernista* novel leads us to another important trait which helps to define the genre: in nearly all *modernista* novels we find the figure of the artist-hero (poet, painter, musician, or sculptor) who tries desperately to define his position and his role within the new Spanish American society of the late nineteenth and early twentieth centuries. The *modernistas* clearly were not trying simply to imitate Decadent fiction, but were attempting to go beyond the Naturalist and Decadentist approach to society and history. They sought a "third way," so to speak, which would help them avoid the hypercritical, ivory-tower attitude of the Decadents as well as the Naturalists' narrow dogmatism that subordinated literature to scientific models and ideological considerations. Indeed, an unprejudiced reading of the *modernista* novels shows that far from being frivolous, superficial, or escapist, they were in fact works in which the *modernistas* confronted not only their personal prob-

4 José Asunción Silva, *De sobremesa*, in *Obra completa* (Caracas: Biblioteca Ayacucho, 1977), p. 187.

lems and aesthetic theories but some of the most urgent issues of their day. If the *modernista* novel as a genre seems vague and ill-defined, it is simply because it is the record of a profound and sustained search for self-definition by the *modernistas*, not only on an aesthetic or cultural level, but also on a political plane.

The very first *modernista* novel so far discovered, Nájera's *Por donde se sube al cielo*, would seem at first to differ greatly from subsequent *modernista* novels in its apparent lack of an artist-hero figure. In fact, the novel's protagonist is indeed an artist-figure, but, unlike most other *modernista* novels, the protagonist is a woman. Magda, the heroine of *Por donde se sube al cielo*, is a music-hall actress and singer, and a member of the *demi-monde*, a term used in late nineteenth-century France to refer to women who became mistresses of wealthy men, and also to the circles in which they moved, which were on the margins of upper-class society. The action in Nájera's novel is set in France, specifically in Paris, and in an imaginary coastal village the narrator names in Spanish as "Aguas Claras" (Clear Waters), which is described like a run-down version of actual towns such as Deauville and Trouville on the Normandy coast. The novel's rather stereotypical plot centers around Magda's redemption (her name is a shortened version of "Magdalena," Spanish for "Mary Magdalene") through her love for the honest Raúl, whom she meets in Aguas Claras while on vacation accompanied by her lover, an elderly senator named Provot. As Belem Clark de Lara points out, Magda may be seen as an allegorical character on various levels: on the one hand, she is an emblem of the increasingly secular society of the late nineteenth century, and on the other, she embodies the hope of a new life based on dreams of ideal beauty.[5] More pertinently for the notion of Magda as an artist-figure, Clark de Lara sees her as an emblem of Mexican nineteenth-century society as a whole, and as a female *alter ego* (in the spirit of Flaubert's famous statement: "*Madame Bovary, c'est moi*") of Nájera himself: "the author [of *Por donde se sube al cielo*] was twenty-two years old, perhaps the same age as his main character, and he was just starting out in life. And although he knew that, being a hemophiliac, he would likely die young, he had hope in the future, just like Magda as she began her new life."[6] Magda's conversion through love from a "fallen woman" to a future wife may be seen as a symbol of Nájera's own often-expressed wish to escape from the worldly

[5] Belem Clark de Lara, *Tradición y modernidad en Manuel Gutiérrez Nájera* (Mexico: Universidad Nacional Autónoma de México, Instituto de Investigaciones Filológicas, 1998), p. 161.

[6] Clark de Lara, p. 218.

demands of journalism into the seemingly purer inner realms of poetry and fiction.

Conversion, as was said in Chapter 2, is one of the major topics of late *modernismo*, and the *modernista* novels concern themselves with how the sociopolitical and cultural changes of Spanish America at the turn of the nineteenth century forced writers to change from being pure practitioners of their art into *intellectuals* in the full modern sense of the term, that is to say: artists, scholars, or scientists who strategically and publicly address issues of political and social import beyond the narrow confines of their disciplines. Most of the major Spanish American novels may be read as allegories about the conversion of Spanish American writers into intellectuals. In fact, the word "intellectual," which in the Romance languages was first used as a noun during the notorious Dreyfus affair of the 1890s in France, first appeared in Spanish in 1901 in the *modernista* novel *Ídolos rotos* by Manuel Díaz Rodríguez. A few years later, the Uruguayan thinker Carlos Vaz Ferreira (1873–1958) would write a book titled *Moral para intelectuales* (Morality for Intellectuals, 1909). But already in 1900 Rodó had begun to analyze, and indeed to urge, the Spanish American writers' conversion into intellectuals in his essay *Ariel*, though without using the term "intellectual." An often explicit dialogue with Rodó can be observed in many of the major *modernista* novels of the 1900s, although the issue of the writers' conversion into intellectuals was already being addressed in the earliest *modernista* novels, such as Martí's *Lucía Jerez* and Silva's *De sobremesa*.

Forty-two years after the publication of *Lucía Jerez*, the Frenchman Julien Benda published his essay *La trahison des clercs* (*The Treason of the Intellectuals*, 1927), in which he took a jaundiced view of the modern intellectuals' involvement with social and political issues, accusing them of betraying what he saw as an age-old tradition of contemplation and dispassionate study. Using a term derived from medieval culture, Benda called these old-style, "pure" intellectuals *clercs* (clerics and scholars) and he defined them as: "those individuals whose activity essentially does not pursue practical aims, and who, while deriving pleasure from the exercise of the arts, or science, or metaphysical speculation, in sum, from the possession of a timeless object, declare in one way or another: 'My kingdom is not of this world.'"[7] In *Lucía Jerez*, José Martí had already described his protagonist, the lawyer Juan Jerez, in similar terms:

[7] Julien Benda, *La trahison des clercs* (Paris, Grasset, 1927), p. 54.

> He belonged to that select breed of men that does not work for success but against it. Never, in those petty countries of ours where men bow down so much, nor in exchange for benefits or vainglory, did Juan compromise one bit in that which he considered sacred in itself, which was his manly judgement and his duty not to use it lightly or in the service of unjust persons or ideas. Rather, Juan saw his intelligence like a priestly investiture, which must be kept in such a way that the believers will not see in it the least stain; and Juan felt, in the nobility of his inner self, like a priest to all men, to which one by one he had to perpetually give account, as if they were his masters, of the good use of his investiture.[8]

However, since Jerez is largely a self-portrait of Martí himself, he exceeds the narrow boundaries Benda sets for the intellectual, and becomes instead a "treasonous" *clerc* – a true intellectual in the modern sense – one who is passionately involved in the political and social events of his age. "Juan Jerez," Martí says, "showed in his pale visage the nostalgia of action, the luminous illness of great souls, albeit reduced by common duties, or the impositions of chance, to small occupations."[9]

The nascent Spanish American intellectuals appear in *Lucía Jerez* as literate individuals who are anxious to participate effectively in the social and political life of their country, yet are unable to do so because of their immaturity and inexperience in the strategies of power and writing that all intellectuals must know. Moreover, Spanish American intellectuals appear in this novel as stifled by violent sentimental and political passions that do not allow them to become conscious of their destiny.

I will say more about *Lucía Jerez* and the other *modernista* novels discussed in this section later in this chapter; for now, I wish to briefly summarize how other important *modernista* novels portray the origins of the modern Spanish American intellectuals and the obstacles they faced.

A very different sort of *modernista* than Martí, Silva offers in *De sobremesa* a still more pessimistic view of the new Spanish American intellectual. Written from a largely Decadentist standpoint, Silva's novel underscores the Spanish American intellectuals' isolation and impotence before the great social and political movements of their time. Like Juan Jerez, *De sobremesa*'s protagonist, José Fernández, is trapped in a chaotic world full of sensations and phenomena that Fernández perceives intensely but that he is incapable of organizing into a coherent system to

8 José Martí, *Lucía Jerez* (Madrid, Gredos, 1969), pp. 68–9.
9 Martí, *Lucía Jerez*, p. 68.

direct his actions. Unlike Juan Jerez, however, Fernández takes refuge in a series of fantasies or dreams of order and power, which give him the ephemeral illusion of being in control of his existence and in touch with his sociopolitical circumstances. Fernández is aware that it is all an illusion from the very beginning of the novel, since *De sobremesa*'s narrative begins after Fernández has experienced a gradual and painful process of disillusionment. From the beginning of *De sobremesa*, Fernández has already come to realize that his life has been ruled by fantasies or fictions, and that, moreover, he could not continue to exist without them. Thus, after forsaking his political and intellectual ambitions, Fernández devotes himself to adoring the image of a woman he loved platonically and who died before he was able to see her again. That woman, named Helena, becomes the purest, most gratuitous and disinterested fiction to which Fernández can aspire, and she symbolizes the utter disconnection of *De sobremesa*'s protagonist from the outside world. In *De sobremesa*, Silva produces a devastating portrait of the Spanish American intellectual as an individual who can not act on his own and who, in his impotence, consoles himself with the impoverished fictions he manages to conjure up in the "somber purple half-light" of the interior (Silva, *De sobremesa*, p. 109).

Despite Silva's pessimism, the events of 1898 and the arrival of a new century led Spanish American writers to decide that it was time to make their moral authority felt, and to try to influence the historical and social development of their countries. Suddenly, in the face of the aggressive foreign policy of the US, it was the *modernistas* – who were used to dealing with cultural issues in a cosmopolitan way – who were best equipped to offer a comprehensive view of the problems faced by Spanish America in the field of international relations. Thus, *modernismo* makes possible the rise of a newly-energized Americanist discourse in Rodó's essay *Ariel* and in many of Darío's poems in *Cantos de vida y esperanza*. The novels of Manuel Díaz Rodríguez display and analyze the *modernistas*' intense desire to become intellectuals in the mold of their French colleagues, such as Émile Zola, Anatole France, and Maurice Barrès, even as they struggled with the Decadents' pessimistic attitude and with concrete circumstances of censorship and political repression. In his first novel, *Ídolos rotos*, Díaz Rodríguez narrates the disappointment felt by a young Venezuelan artist when he returns to his home country after achieving success as a sculptor in Paris. Alberto Soria, the hero of *Ídolos rotos*, has found in Paris the recognition, the prestige, and the authority that, as an artist, he could not obtain in his own country. He returns to Venezuela full of artistic, personal, professional, and even political projects and ambitions, which, one by one, are frustrated in the course of the novel. In the end, when soldiers of a revolutionary army, quartered in the School of Fine Arts, mutilate and defile Soria's most valuable sculptures (a Faun, a Nymph, and a "Creole Venus"), he gives up his dreams and decides to return to Paris, shouting, somewhat hysterically: "My fatherland! My country! Is this my fatherland? Is this my country?"[10] Like Juan Jerez and José Fernández, Alberto Soria is an intellectual who is frustrated in his desire to engage in politics; however, unlike in the novels by Martí and Silva, the social and political obstacles Soria encounters are no longer exclusively embodied in the symbol of a woman (whether a *femme fatale* or an idealized love), but are instead realistically described.[11] Díaz Rodríguez's elegant but flexible *modernista* prose allows him to offer a more thorough portrait of a Spanish American intellectual at the turn of the nineteenth century than that offered in *Lucía Jerez* and *De sobremesa*. Although Soria's attitude does not differ greatly from that of José Fernández, Díaz Rodríguez's morose depiction of his social milieu, with its political parties, its petty intrigues, and the intellectuals' betrayal of their principles under a dictatorship, becomes an important contribution to the *modernista* novels' incipient critical reflection on the intellectual. Alberto Soria's conflictive encounter with the chaotic Venezuelan reality of 1901 anticipates, to a certain degree, the struggle of the lawyer Santos Luzardo twenty-five years later in Rómulo Gallegos's *Doña Bárbara* (1929). Significantly, Soria's clash with Venezuelan reality is so strong that it breaks his "idols," that is, the statues he created, which symbolize Soria's aestheticist *modernista* ideology. The "broken idols" of the novel's title are also broken ideologies.

This breakup of ideologies – particularly the *modernistas*' aestheticist and literary ideology – which took place amidst the great sociopolitical, economic, and technological changes experienced by Spanish America in the early twentieth century, rather than leading writers to embrace the new views of literature and the arts posited by the Avant-Garde, led them instead to delve deeper into the origins of Spanish American culture, seeking to understand and overcome the crisis. This historicist (and philological) gesture presides over the writing of *La gloria de don Ramiro* by Enrique Larreta (1875–1961), and it is not surprising that religion

[10] Manuel Díaz Rodríguez, *Ídolos rotos* (Caracas, Ediciones Nueva Cádiz, 1956), p. 319.

[11] Soria's disastrous relationship with Teresa Farías, the *femme fatale* figure in *Ídolos rotos*, shares space in the novel with detailed descriptions of the intrigues of Venezuelan politics of the time, and Farías does not predominate in the text as do Martí's Lucía or Silva's Helena.

plays here an important role (as in many other *modernista* texts of the same period). Religion in *La gloria de don Ramiro* functions as a metaphor for the spiritual and cultural regeneration and conversion sought by the *modernistas* in the early years of the twentieth century. In *La gloria de don Ramiro*, Larreta offers a novelistic inquiry about the origins of Hispanic and Spanish American culture, but this inquiry is merely the scaffolding for the novel's main theme: the search for a way to revitalize Spanish American literary discourse. As Juan Carlos Ghiano rightly points out, Larreta's Ramiro is a sixteenth-century version of the heroes of the nineteenth-century "decadent" novels:

> The life of the protagonist [of *La gloria de don Ramiro*] wavers between high-flown projects and miserable realities, without achieving a particular continuity. In this sense, he is close to the passive heroes of the *modernista* novels, which the Spanish Americans copied from the masters of Decadentism. The protagonists of José Martí's *Amistad funesta*, José Asunción Silva's *De sobremesa*, of the unfinished longer narratives by Darío, of Manuel Díaz Rodríguez's *Sangre patricia*, Angel de Estrada's *Redención*, and of the early novels of Carlos Reyles, are Ramiro's literary relatives.[12]

This obvious anachronism suggests that Larreta was most concerned not with re-creating "a life in the times of Philip II" (as the novel's subtitle reads) but with replying instead to the existential questions expressed during those same years by Rubén Darío in his poem "Lo fatal" ("Fatality"): "and not to know where we go,/ nor whence we came!"[13] In fact, Ramiro's life, like that of many important *modernistas* (including Darío), wavers constantly between "the flesh that tempts us with bunches of cool grapes/ and the tomb that awaits us with its funeral sprays."[14] It is a tug-of-war between action and contemplation, between intelligence and the senses, between skepticism and dogma. Larreta clearly establishes a parallel in his novel between the Baroque topic of *desengaño* (disillusionment) and the nineteenth-century topic of "decadence." Interestingly, the life of Ramiro spans the last decades of the sixteenth and the first five years of the seventeenth centuries; Ramiro, like the *modernistas*, also lives through the turn of a century. However, unlike Juan Jerez, José Fernández, and Alberto

[12] Juan Carlos Ghiano, *Análisis de* La gloria de don Ramiro (Buenos Aires, Centro Editor, 1968), p. 41.

[13] Rubén Darío, "Fatality," in *Twentieth-Century Latin American Poetry: A Bilingual Anthology*, ed. Stephen Tappscott (Austin: University of Texas Press, 1996), p. 38.

[14] Darío, "Fatality," p. 38.

Soria, Ramiro in the end *does* experience a radical and definitive conversion which allows him to transcend his egotism and to express solidarity with other people. At the novel's end, Ramiro travels to the New World, where he at first devotes himself to brigandage until he meets the woman who will become St Rosa of Lima. Following this encounter, he devotes himself to charitable works, winning for himself the epithet of "el Caballero Trágico" (the Tragic Knight), and he dies from the plague after taking the place of a sick Indian miner in the silver mines of Huancavelica.[15] Ramiro's final conversion is comparable to the a similar gesture by many *modernistas* at the beginning of the twentieth century, from Darío and Rodó to Enrique Santos Chocano and Amado Nervo: after their period of solitary literary experimentation in the turn-of-the-century "interior," the *modernistas*, urged on by the crisis of 1898, decide to abandon the "interior" and the "cult of the self" in order to join the great social and political movements of the time. "I am not a poet for the masses," said Darío in the preface to *Cantos de vida y esperanza*, "but I know that I must inevitably go towards them."[16]

Larreta's novel, like the other *modernista* novels I have just examined, symbolically describes a stage in the origins of the modern Spanish American intellectual: in this case, it is the very instant when the "decadent" man of letters experiences his "conversion" into an intellectual, specifically an "Americanist" intellectual. It is worth noting that, although *La gloria de don Ramiro* offers an explicit homage to the Spanish Peninsular literary tradition, it is no less significant that Ramiro flees from the decadent Spain of his times towards "some region of the Indies, where the plants, the fruits, the birds, the stars – everything – would be new for him, and nothing would remind him of the old and malignant land where he had been born."[17] Ramiro's errancy, from the Oriental sensuality of his affair with the Moorish Aixa and his later attempts to become an ascetic hermit, to his escape to the New World and his final conversion by St Rosa of Lima, may be seen as an allegory of the ideological and literary-historical itinerary of the *modernista* movement itself.

Despite the similarities to the ideas of Benda (who was still little known in 1908), it is evident that Larreta's most immediate model for his vision of the intellectual is derived from Rodó's *Ariel*. In his book, Rodó anticipates Benda's reflections on the intellectual by twenty-six years (although

15 Enrique Larreta, *La gloria de don Ramiro* (Madrid: Espasa-Calpe, 1960), pp. 253–8.

16 Rubén Darío, *Poesías completas* (Madrid: Aguilar, 1954), p. 704.

17 Larreta, p. 250.

Rodó does not use the term "intellectual," of course). Larreta's novel describes the often-haphazard process by which Ramiro divests himself (in Rodó's words) of "the tenacious vestiges of Caliban, symbol of sensuality and clumsiness," in order to move closer to the condition symbolized by Ariel: "the dominion of reason and sentiment over the gross impulses of irrationalism ... the generous spirit, the high and disinterested motivation for action; the spirituality of culture."[18] Ramiro is of course quite distant from the predominantly secular ideals of Rodó, and the literary figure that Larreta definitely wished to evoke when describing the conversion and death of this protagonist was that not of Shakespeare's winged spirit, but of Cervantes's "Knight of the Sorrowful Countenance," Don Quixote. Ramiro, let us recall, was known at the end of his life as the "Tragic Knight," and he dies in the very same year that the first part of the *Quixote* is published, 1605. But Don Quixote and Ariel are symbolic figures that were often used interchangeably, with a similar meaning, in the Hispanic prose and poetry of the early twentieth century.[19]

It should also be pointed out that the *modernistas*' conversion into "Americanist" intellectuals usually implied their adoption of a more conservative literary ideology. As *La gloria de don Ramiro* exemplifies, the *modernistas*' increasing desire to be culturally and politically relevant led the *modernista* novelists to avoid experimentation in favor of a renewed "realism." In the case of *La gloria de don Ramiro*, this realism implied a return to the Hispanic roots of novelistic realism, in works such as the picaresque and *Don Quixote*.

The tensions between the new narrative "realism" fomented by the *modernistas*' "Americanism" and the Arielist concept of the intellectual are explored perhaps more fully than in any other *modernista* novel in *Alsino* by the Chilean Pedro Prado. If earlier *modernista* novels can be read as allegories of the birth of the Spanish American intellectual, *Alsino* is an openly allegorical work that deals, in an extensive and complex way, with the mission and the fate of the Spanish American intellectual. Prado's novel belongs, as a matter of fact, to the waning years of *modernismo*; as Max Henríquez Ureña indicates, Prado belongs to a group of writers who "came to liquidate *modernismo*, although they began under its sway."[20] In

[18] José Enrique Rodó, *Obras completas* (Madrid, Aguilar, 1967), p. 207.

[19] At a parallel date, 1905, Miguel de Unamuno published his well-known *Vida de Don Quijote y Sancho* (Life of Don Quixote and Sancho), and that same year Rubén Darío published in *Cantos de vida y esperanza* his "Letanía de nuestro Señor don Quijote" (Litany to Our Lord Don Quixote).

[20] Henríquez Ureña, *Breve historia del modernismo*, p. 363.

Alsino, Prado summarizes the main issues of the *modernista* novels and tries to bring them to a close.

The symbolic figure that presides over *Alsino*'s allegory is evidently Rodó's *Ariel*. Alsino is a boy who experiences a literal conversion by changing his bodily shape and transforming himself into a winged creature, who, amidst conflicts with his surrounding reality, becomes ever more spiritualized.[21] Although the character of Alsino is also reminiscent of Greek mythical figures such as Icarus and Phaëton, he most closely resembles Shakespeare's Ariel, as interpreted by Rodó. Like Ariel, Alsino's parents are no longer living, and he has been brought up by his grandmother, a faith healer who is called an "old witch" by the people of her village and who seems to be a parody (albeit a positive one) of Sycorax, the evil witch Ariel served before Prospero's arrival in *The Tempest*. Shortly after becoming hunchbacked in the accident that ultimately gives him his wings, Alsino (still deformed, and resembling Shakespeare's Caliban) goes on to serve the old Ño Nazario, a sort of parody of Prospero (without Miranda), who performs simple magic tricks with birds and animals. However, as soon as wings sprout from the hump on his back, Alsino's story departs from the Shakespeare/Rodó model and turns into a perilous pilgrimage, laden with reminiscences of the picaresque novel, in which Alsino gradually attains greater wisdom and self-knowledge.

It is towards the novel's end, after Alsino is blinded by a love potion, that his introspection and prophetic gifts become more pronounced, and he begins to speak and act more like an intellectual. Like Ramiro, Alsino ultimately decides to re-join the world of ordinary people: "To know is not to put others, or oneself, to the test. To know is to coexist."[22] Alsino learns that "coexistence" and engagement with the world are the sources of true wisdom. However, Alsino runs into difficulties in this regard, because, although he already enjoys a communion with Nature reminiscent of St Francis of Assissi's, his wings and his blindness do not allow him to participate fully in human society. Prado symbolizes in this part of his novel the Arielist intellectuals' insoluble dilemma: their desire to move closer to the people, to become active in society, is contradicted by their fundamentally aristocratic concept of culture which posits, from the beginning, an unbridgeable gap between the intellectual and the masses.

Clearly, there was no other way out of Alsino's dilemma than that of

21 Raúl Silva Castro points out various parallels between Alsino and Don Quixote which reinforce my earlier comments about the symbolic equivalence between Don Quixote and Ariel. See *Pedro Prado (1886–1952)* (Santiago: Editorial Andrés Bello, 1965), pp. 86–7.

22 Pedro Prado, *Alsino* (Santiago: Editorial Nascimento, 1972), p. 216.

a new transformation, a new conversion of the intellectual. In the novel, Prado presents this metamorphosis as a suicide reminiscent of the death of Icarus, after which Alsino's ashes remain suspended in the air and are dispersed by the winds. Like Rodó, Prado thought that the solution to the dilemma of the Arielist intellectual lay in the dissemination of the intellectuals' knowledge, a dissemination that implied the disappearance or concealing of the intellectual as the source of that knowledge. Let us recall that *Ariel* ends with a metaphor that compares the intellectuals' education of the masses with the actions of a heavenly sower: "While the crowds pass, I notice that although they do not look at the sky, the sky looks at them. Over that obscure and undifferentiated mass, like the furrows in the earth, something falls from on high. The twinkling of the stars is like the movement of a sower's hands."[23]

In *Alsino* and *La gloria de don Ramiro*, unlike *Ariel*, it is clear that in the end the absent sower is already dead. The Arielist concept of the intellectual ultimately had to give way to a different one which Prado could not, or would not, foresee: that of the left-wing intellectuals who began to appear in Spanish America during the 1920s, such as the Chilean Luis Emilio Recabarren (1876–1924), the Peruvian José Carlos Mariátegui (1894–1930), the Argentine Aníbal Ponce (1898–1938), and the Cuban Julio Antonio Mella (1903–29).[24]

Along with their concern with the status of the nascent Spanish American intellectuals, the *modernista* novels also experimented with the form of the novel as a genre, exploring the various ways in which "artistic prose" could be used to tell a story. In this regard, it is worth examining the *modernistas*' relation to the works of Gustave Flaubert, whose novel *L'Éducation sentimentale* (1869) openly addresses the issue of the intellectuals' often conflictive relation with the social crises of their day.[25] Although the *modernistas* cited many other European novelists as their

23 Rodó, *Obras completas*, p. 249.

24 In his polemical book *Calibán: apuntes sobre la cultura en Nuestra América* (Mexico: Editorial Diógenes, 1972), Roberto Fernández Retamar points out, along with the differences, the continuities between Arielism and the new left-wing intellectuals. He reminds his readers that in the development of Mella's thought, "Rodó's influence was decisive" (p. 31) and that Mella founded in Havana the Instituto Politécnico Ariel in 1925, the same year in which he helped establish Cuba's first Communist Party (p. 32).

25 Critics have remarked on Flaubert's representation of the "uneasy relation between art and social life" in the apparent unconcern shown by the main characters of *L'Éducation sentimentale* for the events of the Revolution of 1848 which were happening all around them. See "1848: Class Struggles in France," in *A New History of French Literature*, ed. Dennis Hollier (Cambridge, MA: Harvard University Press, 1994), p. 709.

models – from Huysmans and Gabrielle D'Annunzio to Paul Bourget and Maurice Barrès – Flaubert's fusion of a symbolist approach to language with the discourse of the realist novel made him a central figure in the modernization of the novel at the turn of the nineteenth century.[26] The diversity of styles and narrative techniques of the *modernistas* can certainly not be attributed solely to their readings of Flaubert. Nevertheless, even a cursory reading of various *modernista* texts reveals that in the genre of the novel, as with Renan in the essay and Verlaine in poetry, Flaubert was for the *modernistas* a tutelary figure who embodied a wide range of ideas about the nature of modern literature. A serious and sustained study of the impact of the work and the image of Flaubert on nineteenth- and twentieth-century Spanish American literature still remains to be done; my observations here are merely an outline of such a research in regard to the *modernistas*.

To my knowledge, only two important *modernistas* wrote more or less substantial essays about Flaubert. The first, at the dawn of *modernismo*, was Martí, who wrote a book review in English of *Bouvard et Pécuchet* (1881) for the New York newspaper *The Sun*. The second, at *modernismo*'s end, was Enrique Gómez Carrillo, who devoted to Flaubert a large portion of his essay "El arte de trabajar la prosa" (The Art of Working with Prose, 1919). Nevertheless, in the collected works of Martí, Nájera, Darío, Rodó, and Gómez Carrillo, among others, one may find numerous scattered and admiring references and observations about Flaubert and his works, and one can also find reminiscences of specific texts and literary techniques of Flaubert in many *modernista* novels, including those I have commented in this chapter.

We know specifically that, besides *Bouvard et Pécuchet*, Martí probably read other works by Flaubert such as *Madame Bovary* (1856), *Salammbo* (1862), *La Tentation de Saint Antoine* (1874), *Trois contes* (1877), and much of his *Correspondance*, of which the first four volumes had been published by Charpentier by 1893.[27] A passage from one of Martí's notebooks summarizes what Martí most admired in Flaubert:

[26] On Flaubert's centrality to the modern, and even to the so-called postmodern novelistic tradition, see the comments by Naomi Schor in the Introduction to *Flaubert and Postmodernism*, ed. Naomi Schor and Henry F. Majewski (Lincoln, NE: University of Nebraska Press, 1984), pp. ix–xvi. In the same book, see also Jonathan Culler's essay "The Uses of *Madame Bovary*," pp. 1–12.

[27] We know which works by Flaubert Martí read because he mentions them in various passages of his *Complete Works*, some of which I will cite later in this chapter. The date of publication of Flaubert's *Correspondance* is found in Francis Steegmuller, ed., *The Letters of Gustave Flaubert, 1857–1880* (Cambridge, MA: Harvard University Press, 1982), p. xv.

> For Flaubert, a writer's style was like marble. He polished it, cleaned it, softened its edges; no phrase left his hands until his thought had fit precisely within it. He hated useless words and pompous adjectives. A synonym was for him a hindrance. His phrases are clear, solid, burnished; a good example of his style is this [phrase] we have placed at the beginning of this paragraph: "One must give authority to the truth by stating it in the most perfect way." This was Flaubert's supreme law.[28]

Elsewhere, Martí calls Flaubert "that sculptor of language,"[29] and places him among the classics: "if by classic we mean any masterly author, in which case Gustave Flaubert is as worthy as Homer."[30] He also compares Flaubert with Baudelaire, and expresses his high opinion of two works by Flaubert that critics have often found debatable: "Gustave Flaubert, who wrote not with a pen, but with a golden stylus, and was never an academician. His neat and robust prose is only comparable to the verses of Charles Baudelaire, and there is nothing in the modern French language better than *Salammbô* and *Bouvard et Pécuchet*."[31]

It is important to note Martí's insistence on the "robustness" of Flaubert's style. In his review of *Bouvard et Pécuchet*, Martí emphasizes the significance of this novel's style over that of its structure, and we see also Martí's tendency to link the purity of Flaubert's style to moral considerations:

In a fascinating note published in *Le Nouvel Observateur* on May 5, 1980, the great twentieth-century Cuban novelist Alejo Carpentier writes about his own knowledge of Flaubert and adds the following information about Martí: "The man who most decisively contributed to make Flaubert's work known to the Spanish-language public was undoubtedly the great Cuban critic, poet, and patriot José Martí, who may be regarded as the most universal intellectual of the nineteenth century in Latin America.... Flaubert died on May 8, 1880, leaving unfinished the manuscript of *Bouvard et Pécuchet*, which would not appear in book form until the following year, after its publication was announced in December by Mme. Aubin's *Revue nouvelle*. ... Now then, on July 8, 1880, exactly two months after Flaubert's death, José Martí, who lived in New York at the time, published in *The Sun* a long essay on *Bouvard et Pécuchet* in which he emphasized the unusual, unique nature of that novel. ... From where did Martí get his information? A mystery! His article in *The Sun* – which he wrote in French, because he still did not have a good Spanish–English translator – gives evidence of the amazing diffusion of Flaubert's work in the Hispanic world, which is still the case today." See Alejo Carpentier, *Chroniques* (Paris, Gallimard, 1983), pp. 494–5. (I thank my good friend Houchang Chehabi for this information.)

[28] José Martí, *Obras completas*, 23 (Havana: Editorial Nacional de Cuba, 1965), p. 92.

[29] Martí, *Obras completas*, 23, p. 194.

[30] Martí, *Obras completas*, 13, p. 422.

[31] Martí, *Obras completas*, 14, pp. 314–15.

> It is a strange book. Pages written with the grand eloquence of a Cervantes, or a Rabelais, and the solid simplicity of Homeric times are extracted from it. We speak of this in no petty enthusiasm. We have studied those crucified lions of *Salambo* [*sic*], the wedding among the Bretons of *Madame Bovary* and the frightful "Nebuchadnezzar," who wipes with his arms the perfumes from his face, who eats in sacred vessels, then breaks them, and inwardly takes the census of his fleets, his armies, and his people. … When a man writes in this style pure, solemn, and vibratory, he is certainly a great writer.
>
> It has always been the style of a master hand, and it is the style in *Bouvard and Pécuchet*. Flaubert hated adjectives. He supplied their places with words so plain that they needed nothing to make them clear. Between two words he always took a long puff of his cigar. He did not walk, because he thought it beneath the dignity of a philosopher. He was wont to say that "Repose is strength." Seated like a Turk, he examined his phrases, turning, analyzing, and pruning them. There were no obscurity [sic]. From truth vigor came forth, and from severity beauty.[32]

Another significant aspect of Flaubert's writing technique which Martí must have known and admired, although he does not mention it in his writings, was the detailed background research on which Flaubert based each and every one of his works. Martí used this same philological technique even in the many hundreds of *crónicas* he wrote to earn his daily bread.[33]

Flaubert's legacy in Martí's work, however, is found not so much in the Cuban's style, which was far more idiosyncratic and oratorical than Flaubert's, but in the structural and ideological aspects of his writings. In *Lucía Jerez*, for example, there are reminiscences of Flaubert in the plot, in the frivolous conversations between Adela and Pedro Real that Martí recounts without comment, and in the contrasting personalities of Lucía and Juan Jerez: like Emma Bovary, Lucía is aggressive and determined in her attempt to fulfill her obsession, while Juan, like Charles, is a comparatively weak individual. As in many of Flaubert's major novels, from *Madame Bovary* to *Bouvard et Pécuchet*, the cast of characters in

[32] Martí, *Obras completas*, 15, pp. 205–6. This text is in the original English (Martí wrote it first in French – a version now lost – and it was translated by someone from *The Sun*, the New York paper in which it was first published).

[33] See Andrés Iduarte, *Martí escritor* (Havana: Ministerio de Educación, Dirección de Cultura, 1951), p. 140.

Lucía Jerez is in fact organized into opposing pairs who end up resembling one another.[34]

Let us recall that the plot of *Lucía Jerez* centers around the relationships among the young and idealistic lawyer Juan Jerez, his fiancée (who, tellingly, is also his cousin) Lucía Jerez, and their friend Sol del Valle. Lucía is engaged to be married to Juan, but their relationship is clouded from the beginning by Lucía's intense and unmotivated jealousy, which leads her to reproach Juan for his slightest delay and his lack of attention (real or perceived) toward her. Lucía's aggressive adoration of Juan seems to border on insanity; for his part, Juan is more passive, and his love for Lucía is frequently displaced by the ethical and political duties that he, as a lawyer devoted to helping the poor, has imposed on himself.

The course of this already tense relationship is interrupted – at least as far as Lucía is concerned – by the arrival of the beautiful and innocent Sol del Valle (to whom Martí refers in the first chapter as "Leonor del Valle": a possibly significant onomastic ambiguity). Leonor/Sol is one of the five daughters of the Spaniard Don Manuel del Valle. By the time the action in the novel takes place, Sol's father has already died; her extraordinary beauty has allowed her to enter the young ladies' school of the city, and allowed her access to the city's upper class, to which Lucía and Juan belong. Juan knew Sol from the days when he bought a drawing by Goya that was part of her patrimony, as a way to help her mother, Doña Andrea, solve the financial crisis which Don Manuel's death had caused for his family. Although, like everyone else in the city, Juan admires the beauty of Sol del Valle, he never shows a romantic interest in her. Nevertheless, when Lucía learns that Juan is helping Sol's mother in some legal matters, and seeing Sol's graduation from the school and her successful entry into the city's social life, she begins to fear that Juan might fall in love with Sol, and begins to feel an ill-concealed hatred toward her.

[34] Jonathan Culler has observed that unlike Dickens or Balzac, where binary oppositions between characters serve to emphasize their differences, in Flaubert: "Despite the evocation of oppositions, as soon as one attempts to formulate contrasts and give them a thematic reading, a great many appear empty, lacking any firm thematic power. Is not Emma as mediocre as the citizens of Yonville? Does not Charles show himself, by his behavior after her death, her true husband, as wedded to the forms of romantic nostalgia as she ever was? Is not the opposition of Homais and Bournisien nullified as they fall asleep together over Emma's corpse? What can be drawn from these oppositions if they can be so easily collapsed? It is not merely that contraries meet, in the sense in which love and hatred resemble one another more than either resembles indifference. It is rather that oppositions may themselves prove empty." *Flaubert: The Uses of Uncertainty* (Ithaca, NY: Cornell University Press, 1974), pp. 130–1.

Lucía's jealousy becomes more intense during the concert given by the pianist Keleffy, when the director of the young ladies' school introduces Sol to Lucía so that Lucía will become her friend and counselor. Tortured and delighted at the same time by Sol's nearness and by the confidence she shows in her, Lucía engages in feverish efforts to ensure that Sol does not become interested in Juan Jerez. At the same time, the angelically innocent Sol, without realizing Lucía's thoughts, resists Lucía's attempts to manipulate her. The crisis is reached when Sol and Lucía, along with her two sisters and the foppish Pedro Real, travel to a country house where Juan will join them later to be with their friend, the painter Ana, whom the doctor has sent there to alleviate her tuberculosis. In the isolated and restricted environment of the country house Lucía's jealousy finally bursts into the open, despite the mediating efforts of the sickly Ana. In the midst of a party to cheer up Ana, Lucía grabs one of the revolvers brought by the male guests and, to the astonishment of Juan Jerez and the other witnesses, murders Sol by shooting her through the chest.

As this story develops, the seemingly strong contrast between the pairs of characters (Juan/Lucía, Lucía/Sol, Ana/Adela, Juan/Pedro Real) begins to blur: Sol's name, for example, evokes natural radiance and light, while Lucía's, although linked to light and vision, evokes the imperfect tense of the verb "lucir" (which can mean "to appear"), calling attention to her penchant for dissembling and her taste for artifice rather than Nature. The ambiguity of Sol/Leonor's name in the first chapter, however, is significant in this context because it raises doubts about Sol's symbolic associations with Nature: Leonor is the Spanish version (through the Provençal derivation "Élinor") of the Greek name "Helen," which means "torch." A torch is an artificial substitute for the natural light of the sun; by using the name "Leonor" at one point in his text (which he never had the opportunity to revise), Martí suggests that there is a basic symbolic identity between the two women. The Nature–culture opposition, which is one of this novel's principal themes, is in fact never fully resolved, despite the fact that the character linked to culture and artificiality, Lucía, murders the one connected to Nature. Perhaps, then, the deepest lesson Martí may have learned from Flaubert is the modern awareness of the utter artificiality of fiction, and of fiction's often arbitrary and capricious qualities, which make it a dubious vehicle for discovering and conveying the truth. In one of his letters, Flaubert defined art as "la recherche incessante du Vrai rendu par le Beau" (the unceasing search of Truth by means of Beauty); a few years later, however, he wrote: "Il n'y a pas de Vrai! Il n'y a que des manières de voir" (Truth doesn't exist! It all comes down to how one sees things).[35] Martí would certainly have agreed with the first statement, and, grudgingly perhaps, with the second one as well.

Silva's *De sobremesa* also owes much to the legacy of Flaubert. Arguably, many of the most characteristic traits of Flaubert's life and work already prefigured and were influential in the later rise of literary Decadentism: an aristocratic concept of the intellectual, a disdain of *bourgeois* values and mores, hatred of stupidity, a penchant for erudition, the artistic valorization of religion, Orientalism, and, of course, the notion of "Art for Art's sake" itself. It is well known that Silva knew and admired not just the work of Decadents like Huysmans or D'Annunzio, but also that of Flaubert. Baldomero Sanín Cano attests that "I was initiated by Silva into the literary currents of our time. Stendhal, Flaubert, the Goncourts, Bourget, Lemaître, Zola, reached me in the volumes with graceful bindings he brought from Paris."[36] According to Eduardo Camacho Guizado, Silva, who spent two years in Europe, lived for a time in Paris, and there he met personally with another of Flaubert's spiritual heirs, the French Symbolist poet Stéphane Mallarmé.[37]

Echoes of Flaubert's hatred of stupidity may be found in a passage in *De sobremesa* where José Fernández mentally addresses, in a comically grotesque way, the other tourists who dine with him in the hotel in Interlaken:

> you fat German traveling salesman who tells of your gross adventures in the taverns and bordellos, mixing them up with noisy guffaws; you slick Parisian with a rose-colored cravat, with your pointy mustache, your pointy-toed shoes, and your dull intelligence, who mangles terribly the English sporting terms with your own guttural pronunciation; you Spaniard, whose unremarkable face and bushy black mustache are always preceded by a smelly cigarette, and who at every moment follows with lust-filled eyes the ruddy Swiss chambermaid …[38]

But perhaps the most Flaubertian trait in this novel is its intensely ironic tone. Silva's irony, to which his novel's diary form and fragmented struc-

[35] The first quote is from Flaubert's letter to Mlle. Leroyer de Chantepie, in *Correspondance*, vol. 4 (Paris: Conard, 1926–33), p. 182, and the second from his letter to Léon Hennique in *Correspondance*, vol. 8, p. 370.

[36] Cited by Max Henríquez Ureña in *Breve historia del modernismo*, p. 146.

[37] Eduardo Camacho Guizado, "Prólogo," in José Asunción Silva, *Obra completa* (Caracas: Ayacucho, 1977), pp. xii–xiii.

[38] Silva, *Obra completa*, pp. 182–9.

ture are largely due, is closer to Flaubert's "epistemological nihilism" (in Eugenio Donato's phrase)[39] than to the selective irony shown by Decadent heroes such as Huysman's Des Esseintes, who is ironic about everyone except himself. Instead, the narrator of *De sobremesa* regards even his own words with irony, as he consigns them to the pages of a diary which he then reads, as an entertainment, to his friends.

In Manuel Díaz Rodríguez's novels an affinity with Flaubert's irony and hatred of the bourgeois may also be found. The Spanish writer Miguel de Unamuno pointed out in his review of *Ídolos rotos* the similarities between the Venezuelan's novel and Flaubert's *Madame Bovary*, particularly in the character of Teresa Farías.[40] Arturo Torres-Rioseco and Klaus Meyer-Minneman have further observed a similarity between Alberto Soria and Frédéric Moreau, the protagonist of *L'Éducation sentimentale*: like Frédéric, Alberto is an ambitious and moderately talented youth, but without great intelligence, who is frustrated in his political and amorous projects.[41]

However, the *modernista* novel that most obviously displays the influence of Flaubert's techniques and style is surely Larreta's *La gloria de don Ramiro*. Larreta, as is known, took *Salammbô* as the model for his historical novel, and closely followed in his own research Flaubert's philologically inspired background investigations. Another homage to *Salammbô* in Larreta's texts is evidenced in the character of Aixa and her Oriental environment. Max Henríquez Ureña has also seen in *La gloria* the influence of one of Flaubert's *Trois contes*, "La Légende de saint Julien l'hospitalier."[42] There is undoubtedly in *La gloria* the same aesthetic contemplation of religious phenomena one finds in Flaubert's texts.

As recent critical rereadings of the *modernista* novels have shown, they are as rich in content and implications as the realist and Naturalist novels of their contemporaries. Besides being works in which the *modernistas* explored the relation between literature and society, *modernista* novels are

39 Eugenio Donato, "The Museum's Furnace: Notes toward a Contextual Reading of *Bouvard and Pécuchet*," in *Textual Strategies: Perspectives in Post-Structuralist Criticism*, ed. Josué V. Harari (Ithaca, NY: Cornell University Press, 1979), pp. 213–38.

40 Miguel de Unamuno, "Una novela venezolana," in *Obras completas*, 8 (Madrid: Afrodisio Aguado, SA, 1958), p. 104.

41 Arturo Torres-Rioseco, *Grandes novelistas de la América Hispana* (Berkeley, CA: 1949), p. 69; Klaus Meyer-Minneman, *Der spanischamerkanische Roman des Fin de siècle* (Tübingen: Max Niemeyer Verlag, 1979), p. 191.

42 Henríquez Ureña, "Influencias francesas en la novela de la América Hispana," in *La novela hispanoamericana*, ed. Juan Loveluck (Santiago de Chile: Editorial Universitaria, 1969), p. 102.

often more daring and experimental in their form and techniques than the realist novels. This in turn led them to become either fragmentary and heterogeneous texts (traits which, when analyzed, give these novels a strikingly contemporary air), or texts which, in their struggle against fragmentation and incompleteness, fell into a paralyzing search for aesthetic perfection. These disparate traits, which earlier critics attributed (with a degree of bad faith) to the *modernistas*' supposed ineptitude when dealing with longer prose genres, may also be seen, however, as signs of the *modernistas*' highly modern penchant for using the novel as a vehicle to reflect on deep artistic and philosophical questions and to mirror those problems even at the level of the novel's form and style. The work of Flaubert served as an important model in this regard, for in his novels one also finds a tension similar to that of the *modernistas* between the cult of artistic form and a radically critical approach to literary creation. Through their novelistic practice, the *modernistas* came to understand Flaubert's nihilistic lesson about the ultimate artificiality and emptiness of literature, even as they struggled against such a view. Flaubert is said to have declared that in *Madame Bovary* he had tried to write "un livre sur rien" (a book about nothing); the *modernistas* could not in the end resign themselves to such a project, and that is why their novels waver between frivolous display and a desire to be socially and politically relevant.

Further Reading

González, Aníbal, *La novela modernista hispanoamericana* (Madrid: Gredos, 1987). The first (and so far, the only) panoramic study devoted exclusively to the *modernista* novels. Argues that these novels may be understood as allegories of the transformation of Spanish American writers at the turn of the nineteenth century into intellectuals in the modern sense.

Meyer-Minneman, Klaus, *La novela hispanoamericana de fin de siglo* (Mexico: Fondo de Cultura Económica, 1991). Broad-ranging and erudite study of the various strands of the Spanish American novel at the end of the nineteenth century: realism, Naturalism, and *modernismo*. Besides offering insightful analysis of key *modernista* novels such as *Lucía Jerez* and *De sobremesa*, this study also allows *modernista* novels to be seen in their proper context as parts of a great flowering of the novel in Spanish America from the 1880s to the 1920s.

6

Modernista Poetry

Until a few years ago, to speak of *modernismo* meant to speak primarily about *modernista* poetry. I have explained elsewhere in this book why this is no longer the case, and how the renewed appreciation of *modernista* prose has allowed for a better understanding of the far-reaching significance of the *modernista* movement in Spanish American culture. Nevertheless, it is true that, at the end of the nineteenth century and the beginnings of the twentieth, poetry still took pride of place among the literary arts, despite the evident achievements of the novel. The *modernistas* still worked in an environment in which the practice of poetry was regarded as the quintessence of literature, and in which all writers were expected to write verse at some point in their careers as a way of showing their literary credentials. Poetry was thus the genre on which a great many *modernistas* (though not all, as we have seen) focused their creative energies. Despite the fact that prose writing may have taken much more of their time (and provided them, through journalism, with a fixed income), it was in poetry that many *modernistas* made a greater personal investment and staked their hopes for literary immortality. If prose was the medium in which the *modernistas* conversed with each other and with their readers about their common aesthetic, political, and cultural concerns, poetry was conceived as the site of a symbolic struggle, an artistic contest or tournament, in which poets vied with each other to achieve poetic perfection and the myriad rewards bestowed by a society that still valued poetry above all other forms of literary expression.

One of the commonplaces of the early criticism on *modernista* poetry was that the *modernistas* were merely gifted imitators of their European (particularly, French) precursors.[1] Today, a more sophisticated under-

[1] Angel Rama, for example, accused the *modernistas* of assuming a "servile imitative attitude" in his book *Rubén Darío y el modernismo* (Caracas: Universidad Central de Venezuela, 1970), p. 125.

standing of the creative aspects of translation allows us to recognize that the *modernistas* were not sedulously copying their French models, but were in fact re-creating and selectively assimilating into the Spanish-language tradition those elements of the French tradition the *modernistas* found most suitable for their modernizing purposes. The *modernistas*' lack of an "anxiety of influence" with regard to their European models was due not only to the complex critical and creative dynamics involved in translation but also to the fact – of which the *modernistas* were well aware – that by the time the early *modernistas* began their poetic careers, many of the major figures in French poetry had departed from the scene: Victor Hugo, the patriarch of French Romanticism, died and received a tumultuous state funeral in 1885, the Symbolist Charles Baudelaire passed away in 1867, and the young Symbolist genius Arthur Rimbaud went into poetic silence for the rest of his life after finishing his *Illuminations* in 1874.

Perhaps it was not by chance that *modernismo* arose in Spanish America precisely at the time when French poetry and prose seemed to be faltering before the challenges of modern textual institutions such as philology and journalism. A glance at the French literary panorama of the 1880s shows that, with the exceptions of Emile Zola, Paul Verlaine, and Stéphane Mallarmé, the series of figures who proliferated in poetry and prose were relatively minor: Théodore de Banville, José María de Heredia, Jean Moréas, Catulle Mendés, Léon Dierx, Sully Prudhomme, François Copée, Joris-Karl Huysmans, and others. The explosions of Flaubert, Baudelaire, and Rimbaud had passed, and only their echoes remained. The ever-observant Martí remarked on this in his obituary for Julián del Casal, when he spoke of "that worthless poetry, full of false and artificial ennui, with which the goldsmiths of Parisian verse have lately tried to fill up the ideological vacuum of their period of transition."[2] In a similar vein, Nájera wrote in his *crónica* titled "Poetas menores" (Minor Poets):

> Isn't poetry dying here and there like a poor woman afflicted with tuberculosis? What great new poet has arisen lately in France? It looks as if French poets are poor because Victor Hugo spent so much poetry. Leconte de Lisle turns Hellenic poetry into French verse. Copée versifies admirably about modern life. But where are Musset's tender cry, Lamartine's serenade, or Béranger's joyful song? There is no more Béranger, no more Musset, no more Lamartine! Every day there are more poets who write lovely, elegant, and carefully

[2] José Martí, *Obras completas*, 5 (Havana: Editorial Nacional de Cuba, 1963), p. 221.

> wrought verses, but every day there are fewer poets! ... Pessimism has not produced in this age a singer like Leopardi. Despair and the tediousness of life have not found a poetic eloquence comparable to that of Lord Byron. … And so lyric poetry is falling behind, and it will eventually become something like the aging mother of a coquettish actress named Science.[3]

For the *modernistas*, the "ideological vacuum" observed by Martí in modern French poetry could only be replenished by casting a wider net in search of new models and ideas; by going beyond the narrow confines of specific linguistic and cultural traditions and espousing, instead, in Nájera's phrase, "*el cruzamiento en literatura*" (miscegenation in literature). At least during the early stages of the movement, the *modernistas* were less concerned with the notion of an absolute originality than with the question of how to build up and strengthen the Spanish American literary tradition: Linguistic, literary, and cultural cosmopolitanism, along with an eclectic borrowing not only from different literary traditions but also from different periods in literary history, were key strategies in the *modernistas*' project to produce a poetry that would be on a par with the very best Europe could produce. For these *modernistas*, "novelty" was a relative value; it was not so much the result of a break with tradition but was instead the end product of a process of accumulation and synthesis of the artistic achievements of past ages: *modernista* verse was to be, as Darío characterized his own work in *Cantos de vida y esperanza*, simultaneously "muy antiguo y muy moderno" (very ancient and very modern). A later *modernista* generation (that of Lugones, Herrera y Reissig, and Delmira Agustini) would reconsider the issues of originality and novelty, and would be more open to the notion of a break with the past.

To a great extent, then, the development of *modernista* poetry may be seen as an evolution from a seemingly pre-modern concept of poetry (and art as a whole) as the imitation and refinement of a received tradition, to the more thoroughly modern view of art as transgression, as a break with tradition. In numerous cases (Martí and Darío come immediately to mind), *modernista* poets showed from the beginning an awareness of their transitional or dual situation: they looked back nostalgically to poetic ages that were supposedly more stable, harmonious, and coherent, while at the same time they looked ahead with foreboding to a new age in which poetry reflected change, disharmony, and struggle.

3 Manuel Gutiérrez Nájera, *Divagaciones y fantasías: Crónicas de Manuel Gutiérrez Nájera*, ed. Boyd G. Carter (Mexico: SepSetentas, 1974), pp. 125–6.

As always, Martí is the point of departure. Martí's poetry can be broadly divided into two categories: the public and the private. The former corresponds to the poetry Martí published during his lifetime, and the latter to the poetry he left unpublished at his death in 1895, much of which, according to his own statements, he was reluctant to publish at all: "I hate works that make us sad or fearful" – wrote Martí in a letter to a Mexican friend, Manuel Mercado, in 1882. "The task of the writer is to strengthen and widen the way – the prophet Jeremiah bemoaned things so well that it is useless to complain about things anymore."[4] The "public" and published poetry by Martí is collected in two books: *Ismaelillo* (*Little Ishmael*, 1881) and *Versos sencillos* (*Simple Verses*, 1891); the "private" side of Martí's poetic production appears in *Versos libres* (*Free Verses*, completed in 1882 and published posthumously in 1913) and *Flores del destierro* (*Flowers of Exile*, composed between 1882 and 1891 but published in 1931). This division between the public and the private also corresponds to a division between two views of poetry and its relation to life: in *Ismaelillo* and *Versos sencillos*, there is an optimistic view of poetry as an expression of cosmic harmony and as an instrument of spiritual and existential renewal. In stark contrast, much of the poetry in *Versos libres* and *Flores del destierro* conveys a sense of existential anguish, self-doubt, a view of the universe as chaotic and contradictory, and thoughts of suicide.

Readers of Martí are familiar with the constant tension in his works between duty and desire, politics and art, faith and skepticism. In recent decades, the stiff image of Martí as both apostle and martyr of Cuban independence has given way to the view of an all-too-human writer who suffered deeply from the stress and anguish of modern life. Increasingly, critics are less interested in the answers this founder of *modernismo* proposed to the political, cultural, and literary dilemmas of his time than in his questions, which greatly resemble those of our own times. Fortunately for literary critics, Martí's devotion to political action and his untimely death at Dos Ríos, even as they fixed Martí's apostolic image for posterity, also left intact many of the contradictions and inconsistencies in his texts. We thus have abundant residues of the *other* Martí: not the clairvoyant hero who sought to free his nation, nor the author of polished and musical verses, nor the orator of overpowering rhetoric and memorable aphorisms, but the anguished individual, the doubt-ridden intellectual who felt diminished by the modern city and who often engaged in a self-criticism so violent as to be almost nihilistic.

[4] José Martí, *Letras fieras* (Havana, Editorial Letras Cubanas, 1985), p. 572.

Martí was less interested in renewing the form of Hispanic poetry than in enriching its ideological and rhetorical resources.[5] As Cathy L. Jrade points out, while Martí showed "lasting respect for traditional Spanish verse forms," he also insisted "that language conform to the lyrical impulses that drive it – even at the risk of being shocking or brutally sincere."[6] In *Ismaelillo*, for example, Martí uses the lively form of the *seguidilla* (a seven-line poem consisting of a quatrain and a tercet), common in the traditional music of Spain's Andalusia region, to produce a loving and near-mythical portrait of his absent son. *Ismaelillo*'s novelty (and modernity) in the Spanish American context lies in its lyrical evocation of childhood's power as a symbol for origins, for new beginnings. Like the Avant-Garde artists of the early twentieth century (from Henri Rousseau to Picasso), Martí glorifies the child's creative potential. Echoing Wordsworth's dictum "The Child is father of the Man" (in his poem "The Rainbow," 1802), Martí exclaims in *Ismaelillo*: "¡Hijo soy de mi hijo!/ El me rehace" ("I am my son's son!/ He remakes me").[7] Notions such as these were virtually unheard-of in the Spanish American context, and their presence in *Ismaelillo* signaled the arrival of a new poetic sensibility.

In contrast to the optimistic ideas of *Ismaelillo* and *Versos sencillos* (where Martí proclaims: "Everything is beautiful and constant,/ Everything is Reason and Light"),[8] his other two books of poetry present a harsher view of existence. Both are written in a freer (though not radically innovative) poetic form, using hendecasyllable (eleven-syllable) lines and assonant rhyme. The longer lines of verse allow Martí to give free rein to his rhetorical powers, producing a torrential flow of images and emotions that seems spontaneous and sincere. The subjects of many of these poems are often taken from Martí's daily experience, including his journalistic work. A revealing instance is the poem "Cruje la tierra, rueda hecha pedazos" (The Earth Creaks, Breaking into Pieces; untitled, the poem is usually referred to by its first line). This grim poem was written just days before Martí penned his *crónica* "El terremoto de Charleston" (The Charleston Earthquake) about the Great Charleston Earthquake of 1886, and refers to the same event, but in terms that are shockingly different from those of the

5 See the comments by Miguel Gomes in "Modernidad y retórica: el motivo de la copa en dos textos martianos," *Revista Iberoamericana*, 184–5 (1998), pp. 457–69.

6 Cathy L. Jrade, Modernismo, *Modernity, and the Development of Spanish American Literature* (Austin: University of Texas Press, 1998), p. 40.

7 Martí, *Letras fieras*, p. 333.

8 Martí, *Letras fieras*, p. 346.

chronicle.[9] Whilst the *crónica* tries to feature the positive consequences of the catastrophe by underscoring how the energy and the religious fervor of Charleston's African-Americans helped in the city's rebuilding, the poem takes a more subjective and gloomy view. The poem's disjointed first lines, with the confusing enjambment "*rueda hecha pedazos/ la ciudad*,"[10] begin with an image that evokes the spontaneous social fraternity caused by the earthquake among the ex-slaves and their former white masters:

> The earth creaks, breaking into pieces
> The city, fear leads to agreement,
> Servant and master join in an embrace:
> The streets are forests of upraised arms
> Begging the Lord for mercy.[11]

The poem dwells mostly, however, on the instances of chaos and destruction caused by the earthquake:

> Power defeated, commanders grow pale,
> The bravest ones turn into trembling examples
> Of deathly fear: weeping,
> A hapless cleric flees: shaking,
> The saints dance upon the temple's altars.[12]

Many of these same instances also appear in the *crónica*. The one I have just cited corresponds to the following passage of "El terremoto de Charleston": "The sound grew louder: lamps and windows shook violently …, a fearsome artillery seemed to roll beneath the earth; the printers dropped

[9] For a more detailed account of the writing of this particular *crónica*, see my book *La crónica modernista hispanoamericana*, Chapter 2. I also offer a more detailed analysis of the similarities and contrasts between "El terremoto de Charleston" and "Cruje la tierra, rueda hecha pedazos" in my essay "Martí violento: de la crónica al poema en 'Cruje la tierra, rueda hecha pedazos' de José Martí," in *Anthropos: Revista de Documentación Científica de la Cultura. José Martí, Poesía y Revolución, "Cuba quiere ser libre,"* 169 (1995), pp. 57–61.

[10] The enjambment is confusing, because it creates a momentary indecision in the reader as to which object is receiving the actions in the verb *crujir* ("to creak") and in the verbal phrase *rodar hecha pedazos* (literally, "to roll to pieces"): Is it the earth, or the city, that is breaking into pieces? As is clear from the rest of the poem, the poet sees in the city's catastrophe a symbol of a broader disaster: that of a whole world falling apart.

[11] Martí, *Obras completas*, 16 (Havana: Editorial Nacional de Cuba, 1963), p. 288.

[12] Martí, *Obras completas*, 16, p. 288.

their letters on the printing-boxes; clerics ran away in their cassocks. ..."[13]

Patently absent from the poem, however, is the whole mechanism of positive and negative counterpoints of the *crónica*, with which Martí tried to bring harmony to his chronicle and mitigate somewhat the horror in his narrative: at the *crónica*'s end, for example, Martí alludes to the birth of twins in the tent of one of the refugees from the disaster.[14] The cataclysm is instead presented in the poem as a sequence of nightmarish images. Also missing from the *crónica* is a shocking scene in the sixth stanza, worthy of a Romantic novel, that synthesizes all the death and destruction caused by the earthquake:

> A bride jumps from the new bedroom
> Where the fresh orange-tree bloomed:
> The groom carries her, dead, on his back.
> He stops, sees the horror as a black cave
> Yawns beneath his feet, and throws himself into it.[15]

The bride who dies while trying to escape from the disaster and her husband who kills himself by jumping into an abyss prefigure the poem's last stanza, which, using the third person (the same grammatical form used by Martí in his chronicles), alludes to an individual:

> ... for whom life is not important;
> One in the entire town! – an exile
> Who invites the towers and porticoes
> To crush his sickly body into nothingness.[16]

In opposition to Martí's attempts to promote visions of social and cosmic harmony and concord in many of his *crónicas* and in the poems of *Ismaelillo* and *Versos sencillos*, "Cruje la tierra, rueda hecha pedazos," like most of his more "private" poems, displays a confrontation with almost unbearable psychic and philosophical depths: a Nature indifferent to humans; an absent or hidden God; a world whose history is turned upside-down, as when the poet asks, in the third stanza:

13 Martí, *Obras completas*, 15 (Havana: Editorial Nacional de Cuba, 1963), p. 67.
14 Martí, *Obras completas*, 15, p. 76.
15 Martí, *Obras completas*, 16, p. 288.
16 Martí, *Obras completas*, 16, p. 288.

> Someone appears: Who is it? Who can, in an instant,
> Drag cities into their own dust,
> Change men into frightened brutes,
> Pour the earth onto the dried-up sea,
> Fling the ages up like sand?[17]

It is not difficult, I submit, to view this more "nihilistic" side of Martí, which seems to coincide with the ideas of Friedrich Nietzsche and to prefigure Sigmund Freud's notion of the "death drive" in *Beyond the Pleasure Principle* (1920), not only as an expression of his modern *angst*, but also as his intuitive sense of the course poetry would follow in a future which Martí would not live to see. Various critics, from Cintio Vitier and Saúl Yurkiévich to Cathy L. Jrade, have underscored the almost pre-Vanguardist element in Martí's poetry; nevertheless, I would caution that in Martí this still remains an undeveloped ideal, and is always in tension with his more traditional and "public" view of poetry as the expression of universal beauty and harmony.[18]

A duality similar to Martí's, although perhaps more extreme, is evident in the poetry of José Asunción Silva. Unlike Martí's, all of Silva's poetry was published posthumously after his suicide in 1896, but many of the poems collected in his two books, *El libro de versos* (The Book of Verses) and *Gotas amargas* (Bitter Drops), had been frequently read aloud or recited at literary gatherings in Bogotá. This is especially true of his famous "Nocturno" (Nocturne), which was also published in the Colombian journal *La Lectura Para Todos* in 1894.[19] The duality in Silva's poetry does not arise, as in Martí, from the conflict between optimism and pessimism, since Silva was decidedly pessimistic in his outlook on life, but is instead based on the degree of openness with which Silva expressed his pessimism, which led to a contrast between the aestheticism and elevated poetic language of *El libro de versos* and the prosaic language and satirical tone of *Gotas amargas*.

Although he mocked Decadentist styles and attitudes in one of his poems, tellingly titled "Sinfonía color de fresas en leche" (Symphony the Color of Strawberries in Milk, 1894), Silva clearly felt an affinity for

[17] Martí, *Obras completas*, 16, p. 288.

[18] See Cintio Vitier, "Martí futuro," in *Temas martianos* (Havana, Biblioteca Nacional José Martí, 1969), pp. 195–239; Saúl Yurkiévich, *Celebración del modernismo* (Barcelona: Tusquets, 1976); and Jrade, Modernismo*, Modernity, and the Development of Spanish American Literature*.

[19] Eduardo Camacho Guizado, "Prólogo," in José Asunción Silva, *Obra completa* (Caracas: Ayacucho, 1977), p. xv.

Decadentism's unconventional and transgressive aspects. "Nocturno" is a perfect example in this regard. Formally, its experimental use of a mixture of verse meters based on multiples of four syllables, along with ten-syllable refrains, explores the limits of the possibilities for structural innovation within the traditions of metric poetry. In terms of its content, the poem evokes, in an elegiac tone, a tropical night filled with longings and regrets associated with the death of his beloved:

> A night,
> A night filled with murmurs, perfumes, and the music of wings;
> A night
> In which fantastic fireflies burned amid the humid, nuptial shadows;
> By my side, slowly, holding tight to me, quiet and pale,
> As if a premonition of infinite bitterness
> Moved your innermost being,
> By the flowering path that crosses the plain
> You walked.
> And the full moon
> Over the bluish skies, infinite and profound, spread its white light;
> And your shadow,
> Fine and languid,
> And my shadow,
> Both cast by the rays of moonlight,
> Were joined over the sad sands
> Of the path,
> And they were one,
> And they were one,
> And they were one long and lonely shadow,
> And they were one long and lonely shadow,
> And they were one long and lonely shadow. ...[20]

Despite "Nocturno"'s unusual form, *modernista* readers still found its musicality enticing, and it soon became one of *modernismo*'s first great canonic poems. Max Henríquez Ureña argues that its verse form became the model for Darío's "Marcha triunfal" (1895) and for the Peruvian José Santos Chocano's "Los caballos de los conquistadores" (1906).[21]

If "Nocturno" and the other poems in *El libro de versos* generally conformed to the initial *modernista* view of poetry as an art that tried

20 José Asunción Silva, *Obra completa* (Caracas: Ayacucho, 1977), p. 20.

21 Max Henríquez Ureña, *Breve historia del modernismo* (Mexico: Fondo de Cultura Económica, 1954), p. 137.

to harmonize tradition with innovation, *Gotas amargas* is clearly a more transgressive, modern-sounding work. As the title suggests, these are brief poems whose novelty lies not in their form but in their subjects, ideas, and tone. Like Martí's *Flores del destierro*, *Gotas amargas* displays a bitter awareness of the modern world's disharmony. Silva responds, however, not with Martí's philosophical and existential ruminations, but with satirical humor, sarcasm, and an openly nihilistic attitude. In a prosaic language verging on the scatological, Silva mocks *Fin-de-siècle* attitudes and beliefs, as in the poem "Cápsulas" (Pills):

> Poor Juan de Dios, after the ecstasies
> Of his love for Aniceta, became unhappy.
> He spent three months of grave misery,
> And after a slow suffering,
> Cured himself with *copaiba*
> And Midy's Sandalwood Pills.
> ...
> Later, disenchanted with life,
> Like a subtle philosopher
> He read Leopardi and Schopenhauer,
> And in a moment of *spleen*
> Cured himself forever
> With a shotgun's leaden pills.[22]

Despite the humor that allows Silva to insert parodies of medical discourse and even of magazine advertisements into these poems, the bitterness he displays in *Gotas amargas* suggests that Silva, like Martí, was not yet ready to make the full leap into a more radical poetic modernity.

Rubén Darío would not be the one to make that leap, either, but his poetic genius and his position as heir to the first-generation *modernistas* would allow him to reflect more openly about his own work and about the status of poetry in the transition to a new century. Current literary criticism of Darío no longer sees a deep divide between his early poems, the best of which were published in *Prosas profanas*, and the later works collected in *Cantos de vida y esperanza*. It is true that many of the poems in *Prosas profanas* share a frivolous tone and an overt eroticism, but this book also contains sober, thoughtful poems, such as "Coloquio de los centauros" (The Centaurs' Colloquy) and "Yo persigo una forma" (I Pursue a Form). Similarly, the introspective, self-critical, even political poetry of *Cantos*

[22] Silva, *Obra completa*, p. 48.

de vida y esperanza also features poems that would not have been out of place in the previous book, such as "Leda" or "Marcha triunfal" (Triumphal March).

An important unifying thread in both books is the abundance of poems that are *ars poeticae*, that is, poems about the art of poetry. By the time he published *Prosas profanas*, Darío had developed poetic codes using erotic and esoteric metaphors, by means of which his poems could be interpreted in terms of an implicit theory of poetry. However, Darío's poetic theory was not as unified as he would have liked it to be; in fact, like Martí and Silva, he, too, struggled with two disparate visions of poetry and literature in general. The one Darío clearly preferred was a sort of literary theology, a religion of literature, modeled partly on Pythagoreanism, but which also made reference to many other varieties of turn-of-the-nineteenth-century occultism. The *modernistas*' esoteric vision of literature posited a pre-established harmony between literature and the cosmos.[23] On the basis of the post-Romantic notion of analogy or correspondences, Darío claimed that literature emanated from the author as the result of a deep agreement between the human mind and Nature. As one of the centaurs states in "Coloquio de los centauros": "Pan joins the rugged mountains' pride/ With the rhythm of the immense mechanism of the heavens."[24] This literary theology logically gave pride of place to poetry as the highest expression of literature, turned literary creation into a ritual, the repetition of a sacramental act, and made of the writer – above all, the poet – a wizard or a seer. To have a command of poetry meant having control of occult powers, and to reach those powers it was necessary to undergo a lengthy and difficult process of learning and initiation. As Darío described it in "Cantos de vida y esperanza" (the first poem in the book of the same title):

> I freed my intellect from lowly thoughts,
> The waters of Castalia bathed my soul,
> My pilgrim heart went forth and brought
> The sacred forest's harmony.[25]

However, in Darío's own poetry there are many instances where a different view of literature emerges: it is the more modern – and more

[23] The best and fullest account of *modernista* occultism and its relation to their poetry is Cathy L. Jrade's *Rubén Darío and the Romantic Search for Unity: The Modernist Recourse to Esoteric Tradition* (Austin: University of Texas Press, 1983).

[24] Rubén Darío, *Obras completas*, V: *Poesía* (Madrid: Afrodisio Aguado, 1953), p. 801.

[25] Darío, *Obras completas*, V: *Poesía*, p. 863.

problematical – view of literature as textuality that the *modernistas* learned from their work as journalists. Darío's erotic metaphors, I would argue, frequently lead in this direction. As is known, the metaphorical equation of eroticism and writing dates from before Freud, although his work *The : Interpretation of Dreams* (1900) aided in its difussion. In any event, whenever Darío and the *modernistas* of his generation dealt with the question of style, that is, of how to transfer their personality, their individuality, to their writings, they did so using erotic and sexual metaphors: "When a muse gives you a child," Darío counseled jokingly in the prologue to *Prosas profanas*, "let the other eight also be pregnant."[26]

Within this erotic metaphor of writing, the act of putting pen to paper is compared to the reproductive act, in which the male stylus penetrates and soils the page's white virginity. According to this "family romance" of literature (to borrow Freud's expression), in which many of the patriarchal prejudices of Western society can still be clearly discerned, the literary work is born from a union in which the orderly masculine "will to style" controls the rebellious, unconstrained, and feminine traits of writing in its natural and chaotic state. Both writing and woman appear in nineteenth-century thought as sources of an original and rebellious vitality that contradicts their apparent passivity. At the end of the nineteenth century, the metaphor of writing as woman was embodied in the topic of the *femme fatale*. In numerous late nineteenth-century texts (including those of Freud and the *modernistas*), the struggle to create a style is symbolically portrayed as an attempt to submit a rebellious or "hysterical" woman to the laws of an ordering discourse that "interprets" woman and tries to "discover her secret."[27]

The figure of the *femme fatale* as an emblem of the dangers of textuality appears prominently in many poems by Darío, including "Coloquio de los centauros," "La página blanca" (The Blank Page), "Palabras de la satiresa" (Words of the Female Satyr), "A los poetas risueños" (To the Smiling Poets), "Yo persigo una forma," "Canción de otoño en primavera" (An Autumn Song in Spring), and "Metempsicosis" (Transmigration of Souls). The *femme fatale* is present even in the first poems of *Prosas profanas*: leaving aside the passive "princess" of "Sonatina" and the cosmopolitan but interchangeable mistresses of "Divagación" (Daydream), we come upon "the divine Eulalia" in "Era un aire suave" (It Was a Soft Melody),

26 Darío, *Obras completas*, V: *Poesía*, p. 764.

27 See Nina Auerbach, "Magi and Maidens: The Romance of the Victorian Freud," *Critical Inquiry: Writing and Sexual Difference*, 8 (1981), p. 295.

who is "malignant and beautiful," and whose "golden laughter" is "cruel and eternal."[28] "Eulalia," "Cleopatra," "Medusa," "Herodias," "Salomé," sometimes, simply, "She," are some of the feminine names with which textuality is alluded to in Darío's poetry. Two others may be added to the list: "The Pale One," and "Death."

In one of the last stanzas of his autobiographical poem "Cantos de vida y esperanza," taking stock of his life and career, Darío declares that his intention had been:

> … to make of my pure soul
> A star, a sonorous fountain,
> With the horror of literature
> And mad with nightfall and daybreak.[29]

The horror of literature: for someone as committed in body and soul to literature as Darío to write such a phrase, it was necessary for him to have seen beyond the mirage of harmony and cosmic order promised by the traditional notion of literature, to confront the more modern view that writing poetry is not a transcendent, mysterious activity, but is instead another of the common occupations of humans in this world.

Although Darío toyed with the idea of a certain *disenchantment* of poetry (like Silva, although more lightheartedly, he tried his hand at writing "prosaic" poems, such as "Epístola a la señora de Leopoldo Lugones" [A Letter to Mrs. Leopoldo Lugones, 1906]), he was ultimately reluctant to conceive of poetry as a transgressive, iconoclastic activity, as the Avant-Garde writers of the twentieth century would do. Significantly, as Darío watched some of the new artistic movements such as Italian Futurism arise in Europe, and as his own vitality was sapped by alcohol and disease, he turned insistently to Catholic religious subjects, as in his poem "Los motivos del lobo" (The Wolf's Motives), about St Francis of Assisi's confrontation with a wolf.[30]

Cathy L. Jrade perceptively observes that the poetry of the last major *modernistas*, such as Leopoldo Lugones, Julio Herrera y Reissig, and Delmira Agustini, signals a "loss of faith in the decipherability of the universe, a loss that marks an essential realignment within *modernista*

28 Darío, *Obras completas*, V: *Poesía*, pp. 766–8.
29 Darío, *Obras completa*, V: *Poesía*, p. 864.
30 Darío, *Obras completas*, V: *Poesía*, pp. 1128–33.

poetry."[31] The loss of faith in cosmic harmony may also be interpreted, however, as a gain in terms of poetic freedom. Lugones, Herrera, and Agustini (particularly the latter two) were more clearly willing to embrace a poetics based not on the accumulation and refinement of past achievements, but on a break with the past, with tradition.

The celebrity that the Argentine Lugones enjoyed during his lifetime has been almost totally eclipsed with the years. Lugones was a late *modernista* whose prolific work spanned the short story, the essay, and poetry. In his deeply troubled life, he veered from one extreme to the other, beginning his career as a young socialist poet and ending it as a fascist. His suicide in 1938 may well have been due to his life's many violent contradictions.

Lugones's poetic trajectory would at first seem to disqualify him as one of the *modernistas* who left (in Gwen Kirkpatrick's phrase) a "dissonant legacy." After a series of willfully experimental books written in his youth, Lugones turned back towards more traditional poetic styles and themes. His first collection of poems, *Las montañas del oro* (The Mountains of Gold, 1897), was written in a combination of prose and verses separated by hyphens (although he never rejected rhyme, as the Avant-Garde poets were to do). *Los crepúsculos del jardín* (Garden Twilights, 1905), his second book, was a collection of poems inspired by Verlaine and Darío in which *modernismo*'s penchant for musicality is subverted by incongruous or ironic images and allusions, and *modernista* eroticism is further intensified. His third major work was *Lunario sentimental* (Sentimental Lunar Calendar, 1909), inspired by the French poet Jules Lafforgue, in which Lugones used comedy, parody, and inventive imagery to exhaust all possible poetic descriptions of the moon. *Lunario sentimental*, in particular, has been seen by critics as the apex of Lugones's project, which was to exalt the power of poetic language and its contribution to the modernization of Argentina. However, after 1910, Lugones's poetry in books such as *Odas seculares* (Secular Odes, 1910), *Libro fiel* (Faithful Book, 1912), and *Poemas solariegos* (Ancestral Poems, 1928) became more traditional and spare in form, and his themes became overtly nationalistic as well as more intimate. In any event, some of Lugones's best-known poems, such as "El solterón" (The Old Bachelor) from *Los crepúsculos del jardín* and "Luna ciudadana" (City Moon) from *Lunario sentimental*, prefigure seminal Avant-Garde works in English such as T. S. Eliot's "The Love Song of J. Alfred Prufrock" (1917) in their depiction of the poet as a mediocre

[31] Jrade, Modernismo, *Modernity, and the Development of Spanish American Literature*, p. 115.

Everyman who is overwhelmed by the tedious routines of daily life in the modern city.

If Lugones's poetry intensifies certain *modernista* traits, such as eroticism or the use of unusual or erudite words or turns of phrase, the poetry of Julio Herrera y Reissig takes *modernismo* to extremes verging on caricature. Unlike Lugones, whose approach to *modernismo* had its roots in his early sociopolitical engagement, Herrera y Reissig's version of *modernismo* takes as its point of departure the Decadentist and exotic aspects of the movement. Born in Uruguay to well-to-do parents in 1875, Herrera y Reissig was forced to stay at home or close to home because of a cardiovascular disease, which would end his life in 1910. To exorcise his boredom, the irreverent Julio gathered groups of young writers in a small room at the top of his parents' house, to which he gave the high-sounding name of *Torre de los Panoramas* (Tower of Panoramas). Max Henríquez Ureña describes what usually took place at the meetings there:

> Not only were verses recited or literary novelties discussed in the Tower of Panoramas, but, in addition, there were also fencing practices with the two rusty foils that decorated the walls of the room. At other times, guitar strumming could be heard: it was Herrera y Reissig, who had taught himself how to play the instrument with just a rudimentary knowledge of music and was trying his best to play a fragment of a Bach fugue or a prelude by Chopin. On one occasion, that group of young men who wanted to live out of the world tried to escape into the Great Beyond, and they held spirit séances, but their main devotion was to literature, and especially poetry. They believed that with them a new age in Uruguayan literature was dawning, and they cared little about the judgments of others who did not see things their way.[32]

Herrera y Reissig's work was largely collected by scholars after his death. He did not live to see his only collection of poems, *Los peregrinos de piedra* (The Stone Pilgrims, 1909), appear in print. In general, his early work owes much to Darío and Lugones, but also harks back to the works of Julián del Casal, whose Decadentist attitude Herrera y Reissig admired. Although he did not seek to break totally with the *modernista* aesthetic, Herrera y Reissig's more playful and experimental attitude was already quite close to the Avant-Garde spirit. He even took the *angst* visible in Martí's *Flores del destierro*, in Silva's *Gotas amargas*, or Darío's *Cantos*

[32] Henríquez Ureña, *Breve historia del modernismo*, p. 261.

de vida y esperanza, and turned it into an object of hyperbolic parody, constantly referring to even more unstable psychic states, such as "spleen," "migraines," "neuroses," "neurasthenias," and "phantasmagorias."[33]

Hyperbole is in fact one of the dominant tropes in Herrera y Reissig's work, along with a penchant for wordplay that becomes, as Gwen Kirpatrick has observed, an eroticism of language.[34] "Tertulia lunática" (Lunatic Conversation, 1909) is widely regarded as one of the most visionary and pre-Vanguardist of Herrera y Reissig's works. In it he used a ten-line stanza called *décima*, which few *modernistas* favored, although it had been popular among the poets of the seventeenth-century Spanish Baroque (Góngora, Quevedo, Lope, and Calderón). Harking back to the Baroque's taste for paradoxes, as well as for the grotesque and outlandish, "Tertulia lunática" indulges in a manic questioning of the poet's own self:

> Things turn into facsimiles
> Of my hallucinations,
> And are like symbolic
> Associations of facsimiles …
> Amid improbable smoke,
> The sugar cane fields line up
> With their military bearing
> Crowned with plumes of glory,
> The weapons of victory
> In an imperial bivouac.
>
> A good-for-nothing Harlequin
> With a senseless tam-tam
> Beats Fortunato's cask
> Upon my worthless brow …
> Dumbstruck is the bell
> That my thought intuits;
> In the echo that flows
> My other voice names me,
> And surly I pursue in my shadow
> My own self that flees! [35]

[33] Jrade, p. 127.

[34] Gwen Kirkpatrick, *The Dissonant Legacy of Modernismo: Lugones, Herrera y Reissig, and the Voices of Modern Spanish American Poetry* (Berkeley: University of California Press, 1989), p. 186.

[35] Julio Herrera y Reissig, "Tertulia lunática," in *Poesía completa y prosa selecta* (Caracas, Biblioteca Ayacucho, 1978), p. 31.

Herrera y Reissig and, to a certain degree, Lugones, pushed the boundaries of *modernismo* into new territory, but it was Delmira Agustini herself who embodied, in a way the other two poets never could, the changes that would dissolve *modernismo*. As a female *modernista*, Agustini was an unheard-of phenomenon. For most of its three decades until the publication of Agustini's first book, *El libro blanco* (The White Book, 1907), *modernismo* had been an exclusively male movement; *modernistas* from Nájera and Martí to Darío and Amado Nervo, despite addressing much of their poetry to a female readership, had regarded only other male writers as their peers. Agustini's poetic talents, combined with significant social changes taking place in Europe and the Americas at the turn of the nineteenth century, allowed her to achieve the visibility and recognition that had been previously denied to most other nineteenth-century Spanish American women writers. Chief among the social changes I have alluded to was the development of an active and articulate feminist movement in Europe and the United States, which manifested itself most dramatically in the struggle for women's suffrage. Another important social phenomenon was the immigration of various European nationalities to the Americas, which transformed the social fabric of many Spanish American countries. The daughter of a well-off family of Italian immigrants in Montevideo, Uruguay, and a feminist by temperament, if not by her actions, Agustini was clearly linked to these two major social phenomena.

Agustini's life was tragically brief: born in 1886, she died in 1914, murdered by her abusive ex-husband, whom she had taken as her lover. The scandal of her divorce and not long after, her death, threw into sharp relief Agustini's double life: the spoiled child of a bourgeois family in a less-than-cosmopolitan Montevideo, she had always behaved correctly and had avoided the public eye (as women were expected to do in that time and place); yet, simultaneously, she wrote remarkably beautiful and profoundly erotic poems in which, like no other Spanish-language female writer before her, she openly expressed her sexuality and her desires. Like Lugones and her countryman Herrera y Reissig, Agustini found in a heightened eroticism a way to move *modernismo* forward and to break with the movement's dependence on prior models from past literary periods. Agustini's eroticism, particularly her emphasis on the body (very often, her own body), was not only intended to shock her bourgeois readers, but also signified a shift away from the erudite, often bookish view of literature held by many *modernistas* (including Darío, and even Lugones and Herrera y Reissig) and towards a view of poetry as a form of creation associated less with the spirit and the intellect than with the flesh and the senses. Her poem "Otra estirpe" (Another Breed) from *Los calices vacíos* (The Empty Chalices, 1913), a book for which Darío himself wrote a poem as prologue, is clearly expressive of Agustini's sense of eroticism as a source of artistic innovation and creativity:

> Eros, I want to guide you, blind Father …
> I ask your all-powerful hands
> For his sublime body poured in fire
> Over my body swooning in roses!
>
> The electric corolla I unfold today
> Gives up the nectars of a Wives' garden;
> For his vultures in my flesh I surrender
> A whole flock of rose-colored doves.
>
> Give to the two cruel serpents of his embrace
> My great and feverish stem … Absinthe, honey,
> Pour from his veins, from his lips …
>
> Thus, lying down, I am a burning furrow
> That can nourish the seed
> Of another, sublimely crazy breed![36]

The new breed of poets announced in Agustini's sonnet included a group of writers whom critics have named, rather unoriginally, as *posmodernistas*.[37] Some of the most important of these were women, such as the Argentine Alfonsina Storni (1892–1938), the Uruguayan Juana de Ibarborou (1872–1979), and the Chilean Gabriela Mistral (1889–1957). Mistral, a direct heir to the legacy of Agustini and the *modernistas*, would become the first Latin American writer to win the Nobel Prize in Literature, in 1945.

[36] Delmira Agustini, "Otra estirpe," in *Poesía completa*, ed. Alejandro Cáceres (Montevideo: Ediciones de la Plaza, 1999), p. 295.

[37] The term *posmodernistas* is used in Hispanic literary criticism to refer to those poets who, while keeping their distance from the Avant-Garde movements that were already reaching Spanish America in the early 1920s, also distanced themselves from what they regarded as the rhetorical excesses and the frivolity of *modernismo*. Eventually, some *posmodernistas* evolved towards the Avant-Garde. *Posmodernista* Spanish American poets also include the Mexicans Enrique González Martínez (1871–1952) and Ramón López Velarde (1888–1921), the Puerto Ricans Clara Lair (1895–1973) and Evaristo Ribera Chevremont (1896–1976), the Cuban José Manuel Poveda (1888–1926), and many others. (This more technical use of the term *posmodernismo* is today often confused with the term *posmodernidad* [Postmodernity], which refers to a new concept of art and culture developed during the late 1980s and 1990s in Europe and the Americas.)

Further Reading

Kirkpatrick, Gwen, *The Dissonant Legacy of* Modernismo*: Lugones, Herrera y Reissig, and the Voices of Modern Spanish American Poetry* (Berkeley: University of California Press, 1989). The best study available in English on Lugones, Herrera y Reissig, and their role in the transition to the Avant-Garde in Spanish America.

Jiménez, José Olivio, ed., *Antología crítica de la poesía modernista hispanoamericana* (Madrid, Hiperión, 1994). The general prologue as well as the introductions to each of the poets collected in this anthology contain much useful and reliable information as well as perceptive critical comments by the editor.

Jrade, Cathy L., "Modernist Poetry," in *The Cambridge History of Latin American Literature*, vol. 2 (Cambridge: Cambridge University Press, 1996), pp. 7–68. Parts of this essay have been included and extended in Jrade's Modernismo*, Modernity, and the Development of Spanish American Literature* (Austin: University of Texas Press, 1998)

Schulman, Ivan A., *Génesis del modernismo: Martí, Nájera, Silva, Casal.* (Mexico: Colegio de México, 1966). Classic study of the origins of *modernista* poetry.

7

Modernismo's Legacy

> They knew it, the arduous alumni of Pythagoras:
> The stars and men return cyclically ...
>
> Jorge Luis Borges, "The Cyclical Night"

Over the past few decades, a return to *modernismo* has been taking place in contemporary Spanish American literature. By "return" I do not mean, of course, an attempt to evoke and re-create *modernismo* as a whole, nor a wish to revive old-fashioned styles and ways of writing. I am referring instead to allusions to *modernismo*, some as short as a few pages and others as lengthy as a novel, that can be found in many significant works of Spanish American narrative and poetry from the late 1960s until today. My purpose in this brief concluding chapter is to present an overview of these remnants of *modernismo* and to offer some conjectures about the possible meaning of the retrospective glance recent Spanish American writers have taken at *modernismo*.

In 1974, two major "dictator novels" were published which contain detailed evocations of *modernismo*: *El recurso del método* (*Reasons of State*) by Alejo Carpentier and *El otoño del patriarca* (*The Autumn of the Patriarch*) by Gabriel García Márquez. Roberto González Echevarría has remarked on the profound reflections on *modernismo*'s cultural significance found in *El recurso del método*, whose main character is a music-loving Francophile dictator of turn-of-the-nineteenth-century Latin America who, among other things, in one of his speeches, plagiarizes shamelessly Ernest Renan's *Prière sur l'Acropole* (1876).[1] For his part, the "patriarch" in García Márquez's novel, although a coarser member of the dictatorial species, nevertheless enjoys the poetry of Rubén Darío. García

[1] Roberto González Echevarría, "Modernidad, modernismo y nueva narrativa: *El recurso del método*," *Revista Interamericana de Bibliografía/Inter-American Review of Bibliography*, 30 (1980), pp. 157–63.

Márquez himself has pointed out that the pages-long sentences of *El otoño del patriarca* contain numerous verbatim quotes from Darío's verses, as well as of his prose poems.[2] The link between dictatorship and *modernismo* in these novels is deliberate: there is clearly a parallel between the dictator, whose authority emanates from his voice, from orality, and the *modernistas*' attempts to attain literary authority by means of the evocation of music and the spoken word in writing.

Nevertheless, already in 1969 the Cuban Miguel Barnet had anticipated in a more general way this return to *modernismo* in his documentary novel *Canción de Rachel* (*Rachel's Song*). In this text, Barnet re-creates the Cuban *belle époque* of the early 1900s while also exploring the dissemination of the *modernista* aesthetic in vaudeville theater and popular songs of the period. If Carpentier's and García Márquez's "dictator novels" examined the ambiguous relationship between the *modernistas* and political and literary authority, *Canción de Rachel* is instead the prototype of a more abundant series of novels that evoke *modernismo* by means of its incorporation into Latin American popular culture. These are novels such as Manuel Puig's *Boquitas pintadas* (*Heartbreak Tango*, 1969) and *The Buenos Aires Affair* (1973), Mario Vargas Llosa's *La tía Julia y el escribidor* (*Aunt Julia and the Scriptwriter*, 1977), José Donoso's *La misteriosa desaparición de la Marquesita de Loria* (The Mysterious Disappearance of the Marquise of Loria, 1980), García Márquez's *El amor en los tiempos del cólera* (*Love in the Time of Cholera*, 1985), Rosario Ferré's *Maldito amor* (*Sweet Diamond Dust*, 1986), Luis Rafael Sánchez's *La importancia de llamarse Daniel Santos* (The Importance of Being Called Daniel Santos, 1989), and Sergio Ramírez's *Margarita está linda la mar* (Margarita, the Sea is so Pretty, 1998), among others.

Modernismo reappears in these novels in various ways: for example, in the (currently unfashionable) custom of reciting *modernista* poetry practiced by one of the main characters in *The Buenos Aires Affair*; in the kitschy style of the soap operas written by the Bolivian scriptwriter Pedro Camacho (who is himself a caricature of *modernista* authors) in Vargas Llosa's *La tía Julia y el escribidor*; in the tango lyrics by Le Pera and

[2] In the book of interviews *El olor de la guayaba* (The Smell of Guavas), García Márquez states that he composed *El otoño del patriarca* "as if it were a prose poem. Have you noticed that there are whole verses of Rubén Darío in there? *El otoño del patriarca* is full of winks to connoiseurs of Rubén Darío. He is even a character in the book. There is one of his verses that I cite, as if by chance; it's from one of his prose poems, and it says: 'There was a cipher in your white handkerchief, a red cipher of a name that was not yours, my darling.'" *El olor de la guayaba. Conversaciones con Plinio Apuleyo Mendoza* (Barcelona: Bruguera, 1982), p. 71.

Discépolo that serve as epigraphs in *Boquitas pintadas*; in the "danzas" of the late nineteenth-century Puerto Rican composer Juan Morel Campos evoked in *Maldito amor*, and in the bolero lyrics sung by Daniel Santos in Sánchez's novel, whose title alludes transparently to Oscar Wilde. *Modernista* eroticism is explored in Donoso's *La misteriosa desaparición de la Marquesita de Loria*. Donoso's novel, which is set during the waning years of *modernismo*, in the 1920s, serves as a reminder that the poetic eroticism practiced by Darío, Lugones, Herrera y Reissig, and Agustini soon made its way to the popular narratives of the Colombian José María Vargas Vila (1860–1933), the novels of the Cuban Alfonso Hernández Catá (1885–1940), and the soft-porn-style novels of the Spaniard José María Carretero (1887–1951, whose pen name was *El Caballero Audaz* [The Daring Gentleman]). The presence of eroticism, along with a great many other topics of turn-of-the-nineteenth-century culture, is richer and more complex in García Márquez's *El amor en los tiempos del cólera*. *Modernista* eroticism is frequently evoked in this novel through allusions to *vallenato* songs, a genre of Colombian popular music whose lyrics often reflected the influence of *modernista* aesthetics.

The late Severo Sarduy's novel *Colibrí* (1985) contains a parody not only of the Spanish American *novelas de la tierra* (novels of the land) of the 1930s and 1940s, but also of *modernismo*, as may be seen, for example, in the décor of La Casona, the homosexual bordello in which much of the novel's action takes place. However, *modernismo* is arguably present throughout all of Sarduy's work, not only in his Orientalist penchant, but also in his overall view of literature, which underscores the superficial, frivolous, and decorative nature of literary language.[3]

A recent literary *hommage* to Rubén Darío is found in Sergio Ramírez's *Margarita está linda la mar*. In that novel, the Nicaraguan author and former member of the Sandinista ruling junta that toppled the dictator Anastasio Somoza in 1979, reflects on Darío's problematical relationship with Latin American dictators, including the Nicaraguan José Santos Zelaya (1853–1919). Through the story (based on real-life events) of a group of poets who successfully conspired to assassinate the dictator Anastasio Somoza García in 1956, Ramírez reflects on the relation between poetry and politics in Latin America.

From a standpoint not limited to Spanish American narrative, it is important to underscore the deep interest in *modernismo* shown by three leading

3 See Roberto González Echevarría, *La ruta de Severo Sarduy* (Hanover, NH: Ediciones del Norte, 1987), pp. 52–4.

poets and prose writers of twentieth-century Spanish American literature: Jorge Luis Borges, José Lezama Lima, and Octavio Paz. Borges, for example, wrote extensively on Leopoldo Lugones, whom he also evokes as a tutelary figure in the prologue to his collection of verse and prose *El hacedor* (*The Maker*, 1960).[4] Lezama Lima reacted similarly to the work of his countryman Julián del Casal, in his beautiful "Oda a Julián del Casal" (Ode to Julián del Casal, 1963). Regarding Paz, his enormous contribution to the contemporary understanding of *modernismo* is found in seminal essays such as "El caracol y la sirena" (The Seashell and the Siren, 1964) and in his classic *Los hijos del limo: Del romanticismo a las vanguardias* (*Sons of the Mire*, 1974).

Undoubtedly, in many of the works I have mentioned, the evocation of the *modernistas* is not confined solely to their poetry but also includes their prose. It is interesting to note that most of the works I have mentioned so far are in prose: contemporary Spanish American poetry seems to be have been less prone to feel nostalgic about *modernismo*.[5] In Borges, Lezama, and Paz, the return to *modernismo* occurs mostly in the context of a literary-historical reflection, rather than as an attempt at poetic re-creation.

Still, we must ask ourselves: Why is it that so many recent Spanish American writers have chosen to remember *modernismo* with such interest and respect? How much prestige can a writing like *modernismo*'s still have, given that to our current taste it sounds so rhetorical, image-laden, stilted, and stiffly harmonious? Why have today's writers insisted on evoking *modernismo*, linking it, rather paradoxically, to popular culture?

To begin to answer these questions, it must be remembered that literary history is not an uninterrupted continuum of works that somehow give rise to one another. In other words, literary history is not a genealogy of texts, but is instead a more complex and discontinuous process of accumulations, ruptures, and returns. Nor should one forget the truism that literature is made out of books, and that these in turn, gathered up in libraries, comprise a sort of collective memory to which writers return in order to find elements with which to compose other books, which are then added

[4] See Jorge Luis Borges, *Leopoldo Lugones* (Buenos Aires, Editorial Troquel, 1955).

[5] Leaving aside towering figures such as Borges and Lezama, whose remembrance of *modernismo* still bears a critical tinge, one of the few instances of an open return to *modernista* aesthetics in recent Hispanic poetry is that of the Spanish poet Luis Antonio de Villena (b. 1951), whose homoerotic-themed poetry and sumptuary style is evocative of Decadentism. See his book of poetry *Poesía (1970–1984)* (Madrid: Visor, 1988), and his essays in *Máscaras y formas del fin de siglo* (Madrid: Ediciones del Dragón, 1988).

to the library in a potentially endless process. Literature does not only feed off itself, of course; many other discourses (those of the sciences, religion, philosophy, philology, and law, for example) also participate in its creation.

Before proposing my hypothesis about why so many contemporary Spanish American writers have shown such interest in *modernismo*, however, I need to mention yet another commonplace notion: Since its beginnings in the early decades of the nineteenth century, Spanish American literature shared modernity's peculiar approach to producing literature. This approach consisted in looking back to prior periods in literary history, subjecting them to critical review in order to derive from them the "raw material," so to speak, with which to create new literary modes. In Spanish America, this modern back and forth movement between past and present, which Octavio Paz called "the tradition of rupture,"[6] is somewhat obscured by the fact that Spanish American literature does not grow solely or principally from its own tradition, but also from foreign traditions that have at various times been incorporated into its own makeup.

Nevertheless, until the late nineteenth century Spanish American writers showed little awareness of this process, since many were imbued with the literary ideology of Romanticism, which emphasized originality and rupture over tradition and continuity. Thus, despite imitating European Romanticism's vogue for Medieval subjects, and despite their obvious admiration for writers such as Sir Walter Scott, the Spaniard Mariano José de Larra, and Victor Hugo, the Spanish American Romantics insisted on the originality of their writings, an originality presumably guaranteed by the different natural environment and societies of the New World. Further complicating this Romantic ideology, many Spanish American writers before *modernismo* did not consider themselves to be primarily writers, but rather political leaders, landowners, pedagogues, and bureaucrats. Their literary vocation was always subordinate to the demands of helping to build the new nations in which they lived.

The *modernistas*, as has already been noted, were the first Spanish American men of letters to consider themselves primarily as writers, and they consciously and consistently advocated for the dignity and the demystification of the literary career. *Modernismo* marks the birth not only of a new literature, but of a new literary criticism as well, manifested in the *crónicas* and essays by Nájera, Martí, Darío, and Rodó. Creation

[6] Octavio Paz, *Los hijos del limo: Del romanticismo a las vanguardias* (Barcelona: Seix Barral, 1974), pp. 13–35.

and criticism were joined together in *modernismo* as never before in the Spanish-speaking world, and thus it is not surprising that the *modernistas* returned, with an intention that was critical as well as creative, to prior stages of literary history: Classical antiquity, the Middle Ages, the eighteenth century, and even Romanticism itself. This helps to explain the openness with which they studied and imitated other literatures in order to create their own. Darío said it clearly in a little-noticed passage from his autobiographical text *Historia de mis libros* (History of My Books, 1906). Alluding to the section titled "Recreaciones arqueológicas" (Archaeological Recreations) in *Prosas profanas*, he states that those poems "are echoes and mannerisms from past eras, and a demonstration to my disconcerted and befuddled adversaries that in order to carry out my task of reformation and modernity, I have needed first to study the classics and the primitives."[7]

My hypothesis is, then, that the return to *modernismo* in many contemporary works of Spanish American literature is part of the normal process of the literary development of modernity, a process in which the *modernistas* were the first to consciously participate. Like the *modernistas*, the Spanish American writers of the decades since the novelistic "Boom" of the 1960s have been "recycling" prior moments of literary history, including the most representative genres of each: the chronicles of the Conquest, the Colonial Baroque, the Romantic antislavery narratives, the novels of the Mexican Revolution, and the *novelas de la tierra*. It would seem that now *modernismo*'s turn has come.

However, the periods chosen for this literary "recycling" have not been selected at random: they are part of contemporary Spanish American literature's quest for origins and legitimation. Just as every great author "creates" his own precursors, as Borges has proposed,[8] today's Spanish American writers have been collectively creating or inventing their own. In my view, the special interest in *modernismo* shown by contemporary Spanish American writers is indicative of their belief that *modernismo* marks the point of origin of a truly modern Spanish American literature because *modernismo* brought about a deep and lasting change in the way literature was conceived in Spanish America. It is not by chance that some of the novels I mentioned at the beginning, such as *Canción de Rachel*, *El recurso del método*, and *El otoño del patriarca*, allude to the transition

7 Rubén Darío, *Historia de mis libros*, in *Obras completas*, I (Madrid: Afrodisio Aguado, 1950), p. 212.

8 See Jorge Luis Borges, "Kafka y sus precursores," in *Otras inquisiciones. Obras completas*, 2 (Buenos Aires: Emecé, 1989), pp. 88–90.

from *modernismo* to the Avant-Garde, nor that they relate that transition to the demise of a certain style of Latin American dictator – the so-called "enlightened despots" such as Mexico's Porfirio Díaz, or Venezuela's Juan Vicente Gómez – and to the rise of a new independent nation such as Cuba at the beginning of the twentieth century. In agreement with Octavio Paz's dictum that *modernismo* "is a true beginning,"[9] *modernismo* is portrayed in the contemporary Spanish American works I have cited as a metaphor or emblem of innovation and cultural change. In *El amor en los tiempos del cólera*, for example, the figure of doctor Juvenal Urbino may be seen as emblematic of *modernismo*'s openness to cultural and social renewal: despite his Positivist education, which leads him to try to modernize by means of science the old-fashioned city of his birth, Dr Urbino also values and promotes the arts and letters.

Needless to say, the concept of *modernismo* presented in many of the literary works that evoke it today is significantly different from that which prevailed until recently in some literary histories of Spanish America. Far from being seen as an aberrant and long-forgotten stage of Spanish American culture, *modernismo* appears in these works as a movement that is central to it; a vital and vibrant movement, whose often-deliberate frivolity and superficiality anticipate many aspects of today's mass media; a movement that, like the Baroque of Cervantes, Calderón, and Lope de Vega, left a deep imprint on Hispanic popular culture, in musical genres such as the *danza*, the tango, the bolero, the Peruvian waltz and the *vallenato*, among others, as well as in the mentality and lifestyles of several generations of the Spanish American urban middle class. Undoubtedly, it is not the harmonious and Parnassian aspect of *modernismo* that is being recovered, but its playful, visionary, sentimental, and sensational side. Not the marble-like *modernismo* of Rodó's prose, but the spectacular one of Martí's journalistic chronicles; not the philosophical Darío of "Coloquio de los centauros" but the tearful Darío of "Lo fatal" and "Canción de otoño en primavera" (An Autumn Song in Spring):

> Youth, divine treasure!
> You leave never to return!
> Sometimes I want to cry, but can't,
> Sometimes I cry in spite of myself.[10]

[9] Octavio Paz, "El caracol y la sirena (Rubén Darío)," in *Los signos en rotación y otros ensayos* (Madrid: Alianza, 1971), p. 101.

[10] Darío, *Obras completas*, V, p. 901.

Today's Spanish American writers seek above all to recover *modernismo*'s transgression of established literary norms.[11] In this sense, the return to *modernismo* may be seen as a "transgression of transgression," for, if the Western literary tradition since the Avant-Gardes is transgressive (that is, based on the breaking of rules and norms), how else can one move beyond such a tradition if not by denying it, and returning instead to a literary mode that favors balance and harmony, that aspires to universal ideals of beauty, but which also leaves plenty of room for sentimentalism and frivolity? After the cerebral "total novels" of the 1960s and 1970s, from García Márquez's *Cien años de soledad* (*One Hundred Years of Solitude*, 1967) to Carlos Fuentes's *Terra Nostra* (1975), and as a response to the political violence and polarization that swept through the region in the 1970s and 1980s, the return to *modernismo* was a healthy return to certain aspects of literature that had been long left aside: a return to a view of literature as ritual, as ornament, and as a means to explore individual feelings and emotions. In *Fragments d'un discours amoureux* (*A Lover's Discourse*, 1977) the French critic Roland Barthes observes that now that the current artistic and philosophical orthodoxy has turned radical transgression into the norm, the positive valorization of a concept such as love (not in its sexual, but in its sentimental aspect) becomes a new transgression: "It is no longer sexuality that is indecent"; states Barthes, "it is sentimentality, censored in the name of what is ultimately nothing but *another morality*."[12] Not surprisingly, then, along with the allusions to *modernismo* we find in many recent Spanish American novels a return to sentimental love and the exploration of the passions – an exploration that is frequently done in a minor key and with a decidedly autobiographical slant.

Like the *modernistas* after 1898, today's Spanish American authors frequently write about themselves, and they do so not in the declamatory, high-strung terms of the Romantics, but in the doubting, critical and self-critical tone found in Darío's *Cantos de vida y esperanza* as well as in many *modernista* novels, from Silva's *De sobremesa* to Larreta's *La gloria de don Ramiro*. A great many recent Spanish American novels critically examine the lives and experiences of their authors: *La Habana para un infante difunto* (*Infante's Inferno*, 1979) by the late Guillermo Cabrera Infante, *Las batallas en el desierto* (The Battles in the Desert, 1981) by

[11] An idea of how transgressive *modernismo* appeared to its contemporaries may be gleaned from Silva's famous parody of the *modernista* style in "Sinfonía color de fresas en leche." Max Henríquez Ureña reviews some of the catcalls *modernismo* received in Spain in *Breve historia del modernismo*, pp. 163–8, 512.

[12] Roland Barthes, *Fragments d'un discours amoureux* (Paris: Seuil, 1977), p. 209.

José Emilio Pacheco, *La vida exagerada de Martín Romaña* (The Exaggerated Life of Martín Romaña, 1985) by Alfredo Bryce Echenique, *La "Flor de Lis"* (The "Fleur de Lis", 1988) by Elena Poniatowska, and *Conjeturas sobre la memoria de mi tribu* (Conjectures on the Memory of My Tribe, 1996) by José Donoso, among many others.

However, unlike the *modernistas*, whose writings displayed ironic self-consciousness, a penchant for erudition, and a fascination with language, today's Spanish American writers are seeking to go beyond self-consciousness and the ironic questioning of meaning. This is a project that Paz called "meta-irony," defining it as "a sort of suspended awareness, beyond affirmation or negation."[13] Paz observes further:

> Irony devalues the object; meta-irony is not interested in the value of objects, but in their function. This function is symbolic. … Meta-irony reveals the interdependence between what we call "superior" and "inferior" and forces us to suspend judgment. It is not an inversion of values, but a moral and aesthetic liberation that brings opposites into contact.[14]

This helps us understand why today's Spanish American narrators tend to view *modernismo* through the filter of popular culture, particularly popular music. Mid-twentieth-century Spanish American popular song takes away the irony from the symbols of *modernista* writing and accepts them, meta-ironically, simply as ornaments of language, thus fusing the "high" with the "low," learned culture with popular culture. In one of his lyrics, the legendary Mexican composer Agustín Lara (1900–70) writes:

> Woman, divine woman,
> You have a fascinating venom in your gaze.
> Alabaster-like woman,
> You are the vibration of a passionate *sonatina*.[15]

Here, the allusions to *modernismo* (in adjectives such as "alabaster-like" and nouns like "*sonatina*") function in a deliberately decorative and superficial way that does not need to be linked, as would be the case in poems by Darío or Lugones, to the world of books and "high culture."

To conclude, in recent fictions by authors of the Spanish American

13 Paz, *Los hijos del limo*, p. 154.

14 Paz, *Los hijos del limo*, p. 155.

15 Jaime Rico Salazar, *Cien años de boleros* (Bogotá: Centro de Estudios Musicales de Latinoamérica, 1988), p. 435.

"Boom" such as García Márquez, Vargas Llosa, and Donoso, as well as in works by a newer generation of authors such as Sarduy, Puig, Ferré, and Sánchez, among others, we see an attempt to go beyond "transgression," to break with a sterile tradition and to reconnect with another, that of *modernismo*, that was able to survive not only in libraries and academia, but also in popular culture and the mass media. It is also an attempt to enter a world without depths, but without deceit – a world of surfaces, textures, color and light, in which, as in the lyrics of the *boleros* and in *modernista* writing, the ultimate truth of writing lies in its appearance.

Further Reading

Kushigian, Julia, *Orientalism in the Hispanic Literary Tradition: In Dialogue with Borges, Paz, and Sarduy* (Albuquerque, NM: University of New Mexico Press, 1991). Deftly traces the legacy of *modernista* Orientalism in contemporary Spanish American literature.

Monsiváis, Carlos, *Amor perdido* (Mexico: Ediciones Era, 1976). A brilliant collection of essays in which the contemporary Mexican chronicler and cultural historian explores the links between *modernismo* and modern Mexican popular culture.

Bibliography

A New History of French Literature. Ed. Dennis Hollier (Cambridge, MA: Harvard University Press, 1994).

Aching, Gerard. *The Politics of Spanish American* Modernismo*: By Exquisite Design* (Cambridge: Cambridge University Press, 1997).

Adams, Brooks. *The Law of Civilization and Decay: An Essay on History* (New York: Macmillan, 1895).

Adams, Henry. *The Tendency of History* (Washington: Government Printing Office, 1896).

Agustini, Delmira. "Otra estirpe," in *Poesía completa*, ed. Alejandro Cáceres (Montevideo: Ediciones de la Plaza, 1999), p. 295.

Alegría, Fernando. *Historia de la novela hispanoamericana* (Mexico: Ediciones de Andrea, 1965).

Anderson Imbert, Enrique, *Historia de la literatura hispanoamericana*, 2 vols (Mexico: Fondo de Cultura Económica, 1965).

———. *La originalidad de Rubén Darío* (Buenos Aires: Centro Editor de América Latina, 1967).

Auerbach, Nina. "Magi and Maidens: The Romance of the Victorian Freud," *Critical Inquiry: Writing and Sexual Difference*, 8 (1981); pp. 281–300.

Barthes, Roland. *Fragments d'un discours amoureux* (Paris, Seuil, 1977).

Baudelaire, Charles. *Petits poèmes en prose*, in *Oeuvres complètes de Charles Baudelaire* (Paris: Conard, 1926).

Belnap, Jeffrey and Raúl Fernández. *José Martí's "Our America": From National to Hemispheric Cultural Studies* (Durham, NC: Duke University Press, 1998).

Benda, Julien. *La trahison des clercs* (Paris: Grasset, 1927).

Benjamin, Walter. "Paris, Capital of the Nineteenth Century," in *Reflections: Essays, Aphorisms, Autobiographical Writings* (New York: Schocken Books, 1986), pp. 146–62.

Biasin, Gian-Paolo. *Literary Diseases: Theme and Metaphor in the Italian Novel* (Austin: University of Texas Press, 1975).

Borges, Jorge Luis. "Kafka y sus precursores," in *Otras inquisiciones. Obras completas* 2 (Buenos Aires, Emecé, 1989), pp. 88–90.

———. *Leopoldo Lugones* (Buenos Aires: Editorial Troquel, 1955).

Calderón de la Barca, Pedro. *La hija del aire*, ed. Gwynne Edwards (London: Tamesis Books, 1970).
Calinescu, Matei. *Five Faces of Modernity: Modernism, Avant-Garde, Decadence, Kitsch, Postmodernism* (Durham, NC: Duke University Press, 1987).
Carpentier, Alejo. *Chroniques* (Paris: Gallimard, 1983).
Casal, Julián del. *Poesías* (Havana: Consejo Nacional de Cultura, 1963).
———. *Prosas*, 2 vols (Havana: Consejo Nacional de Cultura, 1963).
Castillo, Homero, ed. *Estudios críticos sobre el modernismo* (Madrid: Gredos, 1968).
Clark de Lara, Belem. *Tradición y modernidad en Manuel Gutiérrez Nájera* (Mexico: Universidad Nacional Autónoma de México, Instituto de Investigaciones Filológicas, 1998).
Corona, Ignacio and Beth E. Jörgensen, eds. *The Contemporary Mexican Chronicle: Theoretical Perspectives on the Liminal Genre* (Albany: State University of New York Press, 2002).
Critical Terms for Literary Study. Ed. Frank Lentricchia and Thomas McLaughlin (Chicago: University of Chicago Press, 1990).
Culler, Jonathan. *Flaubert: The Uses of Uncertainty* (Ithaca, NY: Cornell University Press, 1974).
Darío, Rubén. *Cuentos fantásticos*, ed. José Olivio Jiménez (Madrid: Alianza Editorial, 1976).
———. *El mundo de los sueños*, ed. Ángel Rama (Río Piedras: Editorial Universitaria, 1973).
———. "Fatality," in *Twentieth-Century Latin American Poetry: A Bilingual Anthology*, ed. Stephen Tappscott (Austin, University of Texas Press, 1996), p. 38.
———. *Obras completas*, 5 vols (Madrid: Afrodisio Aguado, 1950).
———. *Poesías completas* (Madrid: Aguilar, 1967).
———. *Prosas profanas* (Madrid: Espasa-Calpe, 1967).
Davison. Ned J. *The Concept of Modernism in Hispanic Criticism* (Boulder, CO: Pruett Press, 1966).
Derrida, Jacques. *Dissemination*, trans. Barbara Johnson (Chicago: University of Chicago Press, 1981).
Díaz Rodríguez, Manuel. *Ídolos rotos* (Caracas: Ediciones Nueva Cádiz, 1956).
———. *Manuel Díaz Rodríguez*, vol. I. *Colección clásicos venezolanos de la Academia Venezolana de la Lengua, 10* (Caracas: Academia Venezolana de la Lengua, 1964).
Donato, Eugenio. "The Museum's Furnace: Notes toward a Contextual Reading of *Bouvard and Pécuchet*," in *Textual Strategies: Perspectives in Post-Structuralist Criticism*, ed. Josué V. Harari (Ithaca, NY: Cornell University Press, 1979), pp. 213–38.

Fernández Retamar, Roberto. *Calibán: Apuntes sobre la cultura en Nuestra América* (Mexico: Editorial Diógenes, 1972).
Flaubert, Gustave. *Correspondance*, 9 vols (Paris: Conard, 1926–33).
———. *The Letters of Gustave Flaubert (1830–1857)*, ed. Francis Steegmuller (Cambridge, MA: Harvard University Press, 1980).
Foucault, Michel. *Les mots et les choses* (Paris: Gallimard, 1966).
———. "Fantasia of the Library," in *Language, Counter-Memory, Practice: Selected Essays and Interviews by Michel Foucault*, ed. Donald F. Bouchard (Ithaca, NY: Cornell University Press, 1977), pp. 87–109.
Fraser, Howard M. "Apocalyptic Vision and Modernism's Dismantling of Scientific Discourse: Lugones's 'Yzur'," *Hispania*, 79 (1996), pp. 8–19.
García Márquez, Gabriel. *El olor de la guayaba. Conversaciones con Plinio Apuleyo Mendoza* (Barcelona: Bruguera, 1982).
Ghiano, Juan Carlos. *Análisis de* La gloria de don Ramiro (Buenos Aires: Centro Editor, 1968).
Giamatti, A. Bartlett. "Proteus Unbound: Some Versions of the Sea God in the Renaissance," in *The Disciplines of Criticism: Essays in Literary Theory, Interpretation, and History*, ed. Peter Demetz, Thomas Greene, and Lowry Nelson (New Haven and London: Yale University Press, 1967), pp. 438–40.
Goic, Cedomil. *Historia de la novela hispanoamericana* (Valparaiso: Ediciones Universitarias, 1972).
Gomes, Miguel. "Modernidad y retórica: el motivo de la copa en dos textos martianos," *Revista Iberoamericana*, 184–5 (1998), pp. 457–69.
Gómez Carrillo, Enrique. *El primer libro de las crónicas* (Madrid: Mundo Latino, 1919).
González, Aníbal. *La crónica modernista hispanoamericana* (Madrid: José Porrúa Turanzas, 1983).
———. *La novela modernista hispanoamericana* (Madrid: Gredos, 1987).
———. "Martí violento: de la crónica al poema en 'Cruje la tierra, rueda hecha pedazos' de José Martí," in *Anthropos: Revista de Documentación Científica de la Cultura. José Martí, Poesía y Revolución, "Cuba quiere ser libre,"* 169 (1995), pp. 57–61.
González, Manuel Pedro and Ivan A. Schulman, ed. José Martí, *Esquema ideológico* (Mexico: Editorial Cultura, 1961).
González Echevarría, Roberto. "The Case of the Speaking Statue: *Ariel* and the Magisterial Rhetoric of the Latin American Essay," in *The Voice of the Masters: Writing and Authority in Modern Latin American Literature* (Austin: University of Texas Press, 1985), pp. 8–32.
———. "Modernidad, modernismo y nueva narrativa: El recurso del

método," *Revista Interamericana de Bibliografía/Inter-American Review of Bibliography*, 30 (1980), pp. 157–63.

———. *La ruta de Severo Sarduy* (Hanover, NH: Ediciones del Norte, 1987).

González Prada, Manuel. *Nuevas páginas libres* (Santiago de Chile: Ediciones Ercilla, 1937).

Gutiérrez Girardot, Rafael. *Modernismo* (Barcelona: Montesinos, 1983).

Gutiérrez Nájera, Manuel. *Cuentos, crónicas y ensayos*, ed. Alfredo Maillefert (Mexico: Universidad Nacional Autónoma de México, 1940).

———. *Cuentos completos*, ed. E. K. Mapes (Mexico: Fondo de Cultura Económica, 1987).

———. *Obras. Crítica literaria*, I (Mexico: Universidad Nacional Autónoma de México, 1959).

———. *Escritos inéditos de sabor satírico, "Plato del día,"* ed. Boyd G. Carter and Mary Eileen Carter (Columbia, MS: University of Missouri Press, 1972).

———. *Obras IV. Crónicas y artículos sobre teatro, II (1881–1882)*. Ed. Yolanda Bache Cortés and Ana Elena Díaz Alejo (Mexico: Universidad Nacional Autónoma de México, 1984).

Gutiérrez Nájera, Margarita. *Reflejo: Biografía anecdótica de Manuel Gutiérrez Nájera* (Mexico: Instituto Nacional de Bellas Artes, 1960).

Halperin Donghi, Tulio. *Historia contemporánea de América Latina* (Madrid, Alianza Editorial, 1975).

Henríquez Ureña, Max. *Breve historia del modernismo* (Mexico: Fondo de Cultura Económica, 1978).

———. *El retorno de los galeones* (Madrid: Renacimiento, 1930).

———. "Influencias francesas en la novela de la América Hispana," in *La novela hispanoamericana*, ed. Juan Loveluck (Santiago de Chile: Editorial Universitaria, 1969), pp. 95–104.

Herrera y Reissig, Julio. "Tertulia lunática," in *Poesía completa y prosa selecta* (Caracas, Biblioteca Ayacucho, 1978), pp. 27–38.

Histoire générale de la presse française, 5 vols (Paris: Presses Universitaires de France, 1969).

Iduarte, Andrés. *Martí, escritor* (Havana: Ministerio de Educación, Dirección de Cultura, 1951).

Immanuel Kant's Werke, vol. 5, ed. Ernst Cassirer (Berlin: Cassirer, 1912–18).

Jaramillo-Zuluaga, Eduardo. "Artes de la lectura en la ciudad del águila negra: la lectura en voz alta y la recitación en Santafé de Bogotá a fines del siglo XIX," *Revista Iberoamericana*, 184–5 (1998), pp. 471–83.

Jiménez, José Olivio. *Antología crítica de la poesía modernista* (Madrid, Ediciones Hiperión, 1985).

Jitrik, Noé. *Las contradicciones del modernismo: productividad poética y situación sociológica* (Mexico: El Colegio de México, 1978).
Jrade, Cathy L. Modernismo, *Modernity, and the Development of Spanish American Literature* (Austin, University of Texas Press, 1998).
———. *Rubén Darío and the Romantic Search for Unity: The Modernist Recourse to Esoteric Tradition* (Austin, University of Texas Press, 1983).
Kirkpatrick, Gwen. *The Dissonant Legacy of* Modernismo*: Lugones, Herrera y Reissig, and the Voices of Modern Spanish American Poetry* (Berkeley: University of California Press, 1989).
Kronik, John W. "Enrique Gómez Carrillo, Francophile Propagandist," *Symposium*, 21 (1967), pp. 50–60.
Kushigian, Julia. *Orientalism in the Hispanic Literary Tradition: In Dialogue with Borges, Paz, and Sarduy* (Albuquerque, NM: University of New Mexico Press, 1991).
Larreta, Enrique. *La gloria de don Ramiro* (Madrid: Espasa-Calpe, 1960).
Layzer, David. "The Arrow of Time," *Scientific American*, 6 (1975), pp. 59–60.
Lugones, Leopoldo. *Las fuerzas extrañas* (Buenos Aires: Ediciones Centurión, 1948).
Lyotard, Jean-François. *The Postmodern Condition: A Report on Knowledge*, trans. Geoff Bennington and Brian Massumi (Minneapolis: University of Minnesota Press, 1984).
Martí, José. *Letras fieras* (Havana: Editorial Letras Cubanas, 1985).
———. *Lucía Jerez* (Madrid: Gredos, 1969).
———. *Obras completas*, 25 vols (Havana: Editorial Nacional de Cuba, 1965).
———. "Prologue to Juan Antonio Pérez Bonalde's *Poem of Niagara*" in *Selected Writings*, ed. Roberto González Echevarría, trans. Esther Allen (New York: Penguin Classics, 2002), pp. XXX
Meyer-Minneman, Klaus. *Der spanischamerkanische Roman des Fin de siècle* (Tübingen, Max Niemeyer Verlag, 1979).
———. *La novela hispanoamericana de fin de siglo* (Mexico: Fondo de Cultura Económica, 1991).
Miller, J. Hillis. *Versions of Pygmalion* (Cambridge, MA, Harvard University Press, 1990).
Molloy, Sylvia. "La política de la pose," in *Las culturas de fin de siglo en América Latina*, ed. Josefina Ludmer (Rosario: Beatriz Viterbo Editora, 1994), pp. 128–38.
Montero, Oscar. "Escritura y perversión en *De sobremesa*," *Revista Iberoamericana*, 178–9 (1997), pp. 249–61.
Mora, Gabriela. *El cuento modernista hispanoamericano: Manuel Gutiérrez*

Nájera, Rubén Darío, Leopoldo Lugones, Manuel Díaz Rodríguez, Clemente Palma (Lima–Berkeley: Latinoamericana Editores, 1996).
Monsiváis, Carlos. *Amor perdido* (Mexico: Ediciones Era, 1976).
Paz, Octavio. *Los hijos del limo. Del romanticismo a las vanguardias* (Barcelona: Seix-Barral, 1986).
———. "El caracol y la sirena (Rubén Darío)," in *Los signos en rotación y otros ensayos* (Madrid: Alianza, 1971), pp. 88–102.
———. "Literatura de fundación," in *Puertas al campo* (Mexico: Universidad Nacional Autónoma de México, 1966), pp. 11–19.
Pupo-Walker, Enrique. "El cuento modernista: su evolución y características," in *Historia de la literatura hispanoamericana*, vol. II. *Del neoclasicismo al modernismo*, ed. Luis Iñigo Madrigal (Madrid: Ediciones Cátedra, 1987), pp. 515–22.
Quesada y Miranda, Gonzalo de. *Martí, periodista* (Havana: Rambla, Bouza y Comp., 1929).
Rama, Ángel. *Rubén Darío y el modernismo (Circunstancia socio-económica de un arte americano)* (Caracas: Universidad Central de Venezuela, 1970).
Ramos, Julio. *Divergent Modernities: Culture and Politics in Nineteenth-Century Latin America*, trans. John D. Blanco (Durham, NC: Duke University Press, 2001).
Renan, Ernest. *L'Avenir de la science. Pensées de 1848* (Paris: Calmann-Lévy, 1890).
Reps, John W. Introduction to William Willard Howard's "The Rush to Oklahoma," http://www.library.cornell.edu/Reps/DOCS/landrush.htm (document accessed 8/4/05).
Rico Salazar, Jaime. *Cien años de boleros* (Bogotá, Centro de Estudios Musicales de Latinoamérica, 1988).
Rodó, José Enrique. *Obras completas*, ed. Emir Rodríguez Monegal (Madrid: Aguilar, 1967).
Rotker, Susana. *The American Chronicles of José Martí: Journalism and Modernity in Spanish America* (Hanover, NH: Dartmouth Publishing Group, 2000).
Ruiz Barrionuevo, Carmen. "*Las fuerzas extrañas* de Leopoldo Lugones," in *El cuento hispanoamericano*, ed. Enrique Pupo-Walker (Madrid: Editorial Castalia, 1995), pp. 171–90.
Sánchez, Luis Alberto. *Proceso y contenido de la novela hispanoamericana* (Madrid: Gredos, 1968).
San Román, Gustavo. *This America we Dream Of: Rodó and* Ariel *One Hundred Years On* (London: Institute of Latin American Studies, 2001).
Schor, Naomi and Henry F. Majewski, eds. *Flaubert and Postmodernism* (Lincoln, NE: University of Nebraska Press, 1984).

Schulman, Ivan A. *Génesis del modernismo: Martí, Nájera, Silva, Casal* (Mexico: El Colegio de México, 1966).
Shattuck, Roger. *The Banquet Years: The Origins of the Avant-Garde in France, 1885 to World War I* (New York: Vintage Books, 1968).
Silva, José Asunción. *De sobremesa*, in *Obra completa* (Caracas, Biblioteca Ayacucho, 1977).
Silva Castro, Raúl. *Pedro Prado (1886–1952)* (Santiago: Editorial Andrés Bello, 1965).
Sontag, Susan. *Illness as Metaphor* (New York: Vintage Books, 1979).
Steedman, Carolyn. *Strange Dislocations: Childhood and the Idea of Human Interiority, 1780–1930* (London: Virago Press, 1995).
The Cambridge History of Latin American Literature, vol. 2. Ed. Enrique Pupo-Walker and Roberto González Echevarría (Cambridge: Cambridge University Press, 1996).
Torres-Rioseco, Arturo. *Grandes novelistas de la América Hispana* (Berkeley, U of California P, 1949).
Unamuno, Miguel de. "Una novela venezolana" in *Obras completas*, 8 (Madrid: Afrodisio Aguado, 1958), pp. 104–16.
Uslar Pietri, Arturo. *Breve historia de la novela hispanoamericana* (Caracas: Ediciones Edime, 1954).
Villena, Luis Antonio de. *Máscaras y formas del fin de siglo* (Madrid: Ediciones del Dragón, 1988).
———. *Poesía (1970–1984)* (Madrid: Visor, 1988).
Vitier, Cintio. "Martí futuro," in *Temas martianos* (Havana: Biblioteca Nacional José Martí, 1969), pp. 195–239.
Yurkiévich, Saúl. *Celebración del modernismo* (Barcelona: Tusquets, 1976).

INDEX